DAN SATER'S
Country Estates
HOME PLANS

A DESIGNS DIRECT PUBLISHING BOOK

Presented by

The Sater Design Collection, Inc.
The Center at the Springs
25241 Elementary Way, Suite 201, Bonita Springs, FL 34135

Dan F. Sater, II — CEO and Author

Rickard Bailey — Editor-in-Chief

Jennifer Baker — Editor

CONTRIBUTING WRITERS

Laura Hurst Brown, Alan Lopuszynski, Matt McGarry, Clare Ulik

Dave Jenkins — Illustrator

Patrick Chin Shue — Production Illustrator

Concept Visualization, Inc. — Virtual Illustrator

Diane Zwack — Creative Director/Art Director

Kim Campeau — Graphic Artist

Emily Sessa — Graphic Artist

CONTRIBUTING PHOTOGRAPHERS

Tom Harper, Laurence Taylor,
Doug Thompson, Oscar Thompson and CJ Walker

Front Cover Photo: Doug Thompson
Back Cover Photos: CJ Walker, Doug Thompson
Front Flap Image: Concept Visualization, Inc.

Printed by: Toppan Printing Co., Hong Kong

First Printing: February 2007

10 9 8 7 6 5 4 3 2 1

PHOTOGRAPH BY: CJ WALKER

Contents

7076 | *Cadenwood*

FRONT VIEW

Sure to catch the attention of neighbors passing by, a triple-window dormer resides over the charming wraparound porch. Timeless columns, decorative shutters and a sunburst transom over the front door reflect the high quality craftsmanship that continues inside.

DINING ROOM

A step-up tray ceiling and crisp white crown molding lend a handcrafted touch to the formal dining room. Located next to the foyer, diners will enjoy moonlight views past the front porch while the host will appreciate the convenience of the nearby kitchen.

Country Oasis

A serene retreat from the hectic pace of everyday life.

An inviting wraparound porch announces the relaxed ambience of the interior, while the symmetry of a series of classic columns and a triple-window dormer perfect the curb appeal of the façade. Built-in cabinetry, a fireplace and a series of French doors highlight the great room, which also features a wet bar.

To the right of the plan, an island kitchen establishes a link between the nook and the main living area, and easily serves the formal dining room. Bay windows bring in natural light along the rear perimeter, which connects to the outdoors via a covered porch and terrace that step down into the property.

The upper level boasts a catwalk that connects two secondary suites with a staircase that leads to a sizeable bonus room above the garage. Both of the guest bedrooms open to a rear deck, which overlooks the pool and spa area.

GREAT ROOM VIEWS

As you pass through the foyer and under the second-floor bridge, you're greeted by the warmth and beauty of the great room. Deeply carved coffers serve as home to a pair of armoires that bookend the fireplace. A second-floor balcony provides access to the guest suites and, at the same time, a "scenic overlook" of the great room and foyer.

KITCHEN

A wraparound eating bar, breakfast nook, walk-in pantry and center prep island are just a few of the features that make the kitchen cozy and, at the same time, efficient. A box-beam ceiling, warm color palette and hardwood floors come together perfectly to enhance the inviting atmosphere.

MEDIA/BONUS ROOM

This spacious bonus room is perfectly designed to accommodate the latest multi-media equipment, friends and family will love "going to the movies" at your house.

FABRIC CARE STUDIO

Conveniently located directly off of the garage, the Fabric Care Studio features the DryAire™ Drying Cabinet and Duet® Washer and Dryer. This pair of laundry appliances makes optimal use of your time caring for fabrics with its ENERGY STAR® qualified performance.

VERANDAH

An abundance of outdoor entertaining areas—outdoor kitchen, pool, spa, and multiple places to pull up a chair—makes the verandah the perfect place for enjoying the great outdoors with the company of friends and family.

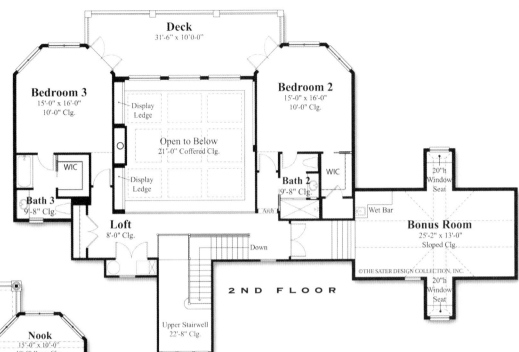

Deck
31'-6" x 10'-0"

Bedroom 3
15'-0" x 16'-0"
10'-0" Clg.

Display Ledge

Open to Below
21'-0" Coffered Clg.

Display Ledge

WIC

Bath 3
9'-8" Clg.

Bedroom 2
15'-0" x 16'-0"
10'-0" Clg.

Bath 2
9'-8" Clg.

WIC

Wet Bar

Arch

20"h Window Seat

Bonus Room
25'-2" x 13'-0"
Sloped Clg.

Loft
8'-0" Clg.

Down

©THE SATER DESIGN COLLECTION, INC.

20"h Window Seat

Upper Stairwell
22'-8" Clg.

2ND FLOOR

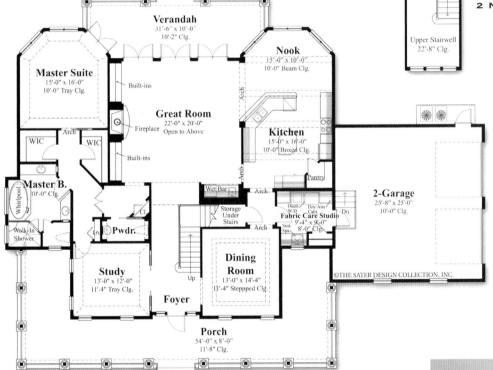

Verandah
31'-6" x 10'-0"
10'-2" Clg.

Master Suite
15'-0" x 16'-0"
10'-0" Tray Clg.

Built-ins

Great Room
22'-0" x 20'-0"
Open to Above

Fireplace

Built-ins

Nook
15'-0" x 10'-0"
10'-0" Beam Clg.

Kitchen
15'-0" x 16'-0"
10'-0" Boxed Clg.

WIC   WIC

Arch

Pantry

Master B.
10'-0" Clg.

Whirlpool

Walk-In Shower

Wet Bar

Storage Under Stairs

Fabric Care Studio
9'-4" x 9'-0"
8'-0" Clg.

Duct W/D Dry-Aire Cabt.

Sink Spa

Arch

Arch

Dn

2-Garage
25'-8" x 25'-0"
10'-0" Clg.

Pwdr.

Cl.

Up

Study
13'-0" x 12'-0"
11'-4" Tray Clg.

Dining Room
13'-0" x 14'-4"
11'-4" Steppped Clg.

Foyer

©THE SATER DESIGN COLLECTION, INC.

Porch
54'-0" x 8'-0"
11'-8" Clg.

1ST FLOOR

7076 | *Cadenwood*

3 Bedroom

3-1/2 Bath

1st Floor: **2,253** sq ft

2nd Floor: **1,510** sq ft

Living Area: **3,763** sq ft

Width: **77'2"**

Depth: **64'0"**

Exterior Walls: **2x6**

Foundation: crawl space

Price Code: **C4**

REAR VIEW

Multiple windows and glass doors create a seamless connection between the interior and outdoor living spaces.

Genteel by Nature

Enjoy multiple connections with the outdoors.

Triple sets of double glass doors invite the sun to pour into the foyer, dining room and study of this view-oriented design. Initially, your eye may be drawn to this country estate's impressive façade with its classic hipped rooflines, twin dormers and graceful slump arches. But, past the front porch awaits an intimate retreat where friends and family alike will enjoy spending their downtime.

The open nature of the floor plan allows fresh breezes to move freely through the dining room to the living room, kitchen nook and leisure room—each one leading smoothly to the next past hand-crafted pillars and through elegantly arched doorways. Retreating glass doors further extend the living space outward, providing a seamless connection from the leisure and living rooms to the lanai.

On the left wing of the home, an arched entryway with built-ins leads to two private bedrooms featuring walk-in closets and a "Jack-and-Jill" bath. Located on the opposite wing, a private foyer opens to the luxurious master suite that offers seclusion, relaxation and contentment.

FRONT VIEW

Wide, expressive arches meet you as you approach, receiving you through a high, double-door entryway and porch area. Stately pillars and tall, arched windows complete the warm and comfortable welcome.

LEISURE ROOM

Here's where relaxation meets congregation. Close to the nook, open to the kitchen and spilling out into a back-yard pool area and beyond, the family room will become both the center of your home's activity as well as its most comfy area of respite.

LIVING ROOM

High, stepped ceilings, attractive built-ins and a peaceful fireplace hearth all add to your feelings of warmth and contentment in the living room. Depending on where you're comfortably sitting, the living room affords open views of both the formal and informal living areas.

KITCHEN

The inviting, open kitchen provides an ideal area to entertain, gather, relax—and cook, of course! With a cozy eating bar and easy access to the dining room, the kitchen is every bit as convenient as it is comfy.

DINING ROOM

This exquisite, formal dining room is set off by paneled decorative columns, a beamed stepped ceiling and is open to the foyer, kitchen and living room through attractive, arched doorways.

MASTER BATH

Private, well-appointed and spacious, the master bath offers a strong feeling of tranquility and comfort. Just outside the windows, a private master garden enhances the spa-like quality of the room.

MASTER BEDROOM

Accessed through its own foyer and arched doorways, you'll find peace and quiet in this generously-sized master bedroom. At the same time, you'll feel close to the outside world through a set of double doors, opening to the lanai and beyond.

©THE SATER DESIGN COLLECTION, INC.

7080 | *Manchester*

4 Bedroom

3-1/2 Bath

Living Area: **3,331** sq ft

Width: **68'8"**

Depth: **106'0"**

Exterior Walls: **2x6**

Foundation: crawl space

Price Code: **C4**

REAR VIEW

An expansive outdoor living space, the lanai enjoys a fluid connection with the living and leisure rooms through retreating glass doors. An outdoor grill and pool area lure friends and family outside to enjoy an evening under the stars.

Open Invitation

Beautifully designed both inside and out.

Open and inviting, this Victorian-inspired home offers a generous interior with flexible rooms and a seamless boundary with the outdoors. Shingles, fretwork and clapboard siding lend charm to the informal spirit of the exterior, and set the tone for a relaxed décor inside.

The foyer opens to the great room, which is centered by a high coffered ceiling and a brick fireplace. Ideal for relaxing, the great room also features a wall of glass doors that open outside to a covered porch. Arches define the casual living spaces, accenting bookcases and an open counter shared by the main kitchen. Arranged to provide cozy places to entertain, this open living space can easily host an intimate evening for two or an elaborate party.

A split floor plan ensures privacy for guests and homeowners alike. The right side includes a powder room, laundry room and two secondary bedrooms. Bordering the left wing is a study and spacious master suite.

7051 | *Bainbridge*

FRONT VIEW

The classic front porch has an abundance of windows that reflect natural light by day and radiate a golden glow at night. A prominent central gable establishes the street presence of the façade and works with a layered elevation to enhance the curb appeal of the home.

KITCHEN

A natural gathering place, the kitchen combines function with comfort. A stainless-steel double oven, center prep island and plenty of storage space will please cooks of all levels. The nook and eating bar provide relaxing areas for hungry appetites. The laundry and dining room are conveniently located just through the archway.

DINING ROOM

A stylish stepped, tin ceiling emphasizes the formality of the dining room. Defined by columns, the dining room is located near the kitchen and offers "patrons" front porch views.

GREAT ROOM VIEWS

Three sets of glass doors and repeating arches opening to the kitchen add charm to the generous great room. Molded columns flank a cabinet-style eating bar, perfect for quick snacks and conversations with the cook. A sculpted fireplace, built-in cabinetry and a beamed coffered ceiling add a nice, handcrafted touch.

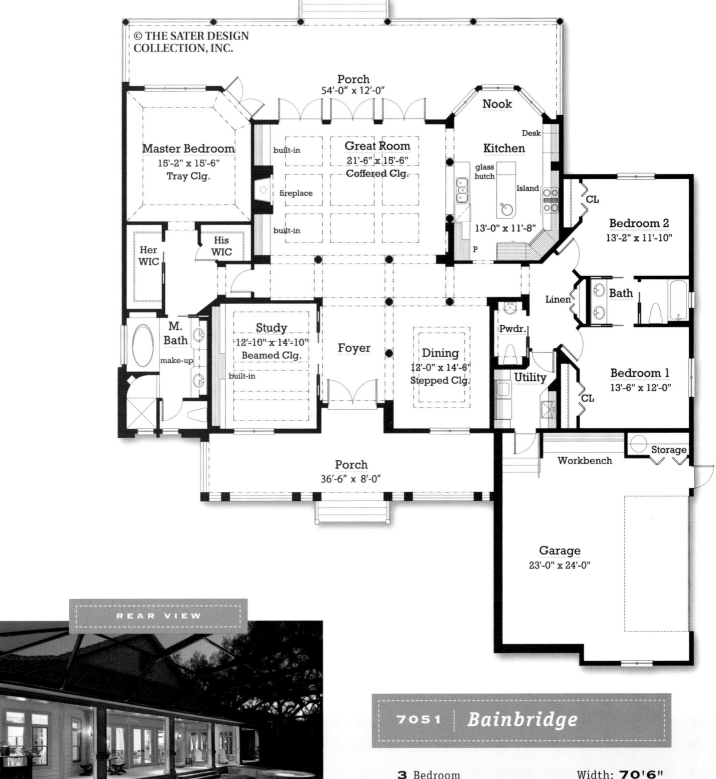

© THE SATER DESIGN COLLECTION, INC.

Porch
54'-0" x 12'-0"

Nook

Desk

Master Bedroom
15'-2" x 15'-6"
Tray Clg.

built-in

Great Room
21'-6" x 15'-6"
Coffered Clg.

Kitchen

glass
hutch

Island

CL

Bedroom 2
13'-2" x 11'-10"

fireplace

built-in

13'-0" x 11'-8"

P

Her
WIC

His
WIC

Bath

Linen

M.
Bath

make-up

Study
12'-10" x 14'-10"
Beamed Clg.

built-in

Foyer

Dining
12'-0" x 14'-6"
Stepped Clg.

Pwdr.

Utility

Bedroom 1
13'-6" x 12'-0"

CL

Porch
36'-6" x 8'-0"

Workbench

Storage

Garage
23'-0" x 24'-0"

REAR VIEW

7051 | *Bainbridge*

The warm ambiance of the back porch creates the ideal setting for outdoor occasions with family and friends.

3 Bedroom

2-1/2 Bath

Living Area: **2,555** sq ft

Width: **70'6"**

Depth: **76'6"**

Exterior Walls: **2x6**

Foundation: crawl space

Price Code: **C3**

Nostalgic Estate

Strong ties to the past seamlessly connect with modern amenities.

Nothing speaks charm and invitation like a front porch, and the portico of this uniquely designed estate offers limitless potential for memorable events—large and small. The foyer opens up to the living room, where oversized bay windows welcome in outdoor views and light. The room's open connections to other living areas of the home creates a natural gathering spot.

The well-thought-out floor plan allots one entire side of the home to a sizeable master retreat and dedicates the other to a flexible leisure room/kitchen/breakfast nook common area. Designed with friends and family in mind, the leisure room is a comfy gathering place. The kitchen is a gourmet chef's—and busy family's—delight with its double island and abundant workplace for multiple cooks. An oversized lanai wraps the back of the home, where every room has access and views via French doors, oversized windows or disappearing glass walls.

6781 | *Rosemary Bay*

FRONT VIEW

Square columns and multi-pane windows add to the simple style of the front porch, while the striking cupola grabs the attention of those who pass by. Whether or not to add a couple of rocking chairs is up to you.

LIVING ROOM

A trio of floor-to-ceiling windows invites the outdoors in to the stylish, yet comfortable living room. A gracious spot for enjoying company, the living room is complemented by a powder bath located down the hall, and the formal dining room just steps away.

DINING ROOM

Enjoy candlelight dinners in the octagonal-shaped dining room, with bay windows offering views of the front yard. Entertaining is easy with the kitchen and wet bar located conveniently near by. A built-in niche and stepped ceiling add character to the room.

STUDY

French doors lead into the quiet solitude of the study. Built-in cabinetry, a stepped ceiling and bay windows are perfect examples of the attention to detail that went into the design of this home.

KITCHEN

Multiple workstations, a large walk-in pantry and built-in work desk create a kitchen that is both functional and comfortable. Opening up to the nook and leisure room, the kitchen is a bright and airy spot to unwind and catch up with the family.

MASTER BEDROOM

A welcoming haven, the master retreat encompasses the entire left wing of the home. Arches line the foyer leading to the master suite where a cozy sitting nook and French doors to the lanai indulge the need for privacy.

MASTER BATH

Comfort and relaxation are a few steps away in the generous master bath. A walk-in shower, whirlpool tub and dual vanities create a spa-like atmosphere.

KITCHEN/LEISURE ROOM

The leisure room and kitchen flow seamlessly into one another and create a welcoming environment.

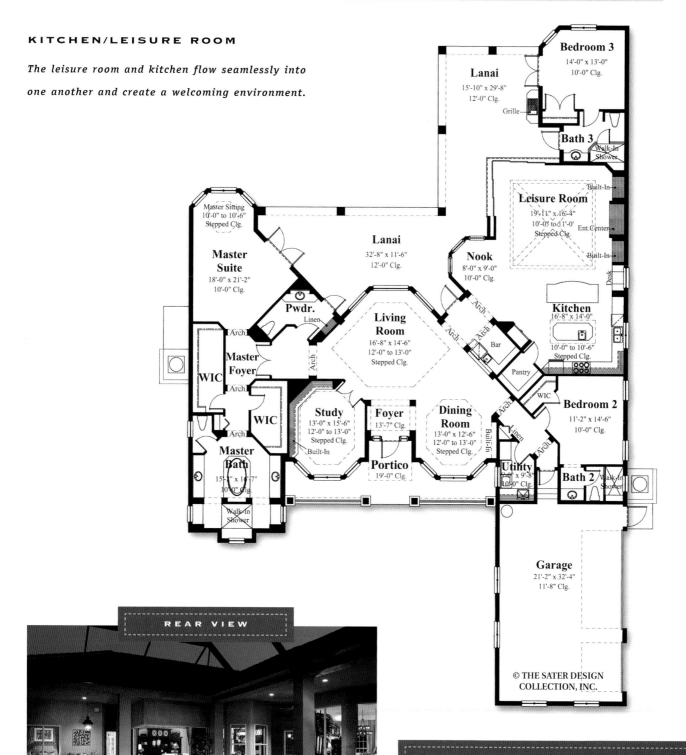

Bedroom 3
14'-0" x 13'-0"
10'-0" Clg.

Lanai
15'-10" x 29'-8"
12'-0" Clg.

Grille

Bath 3
Walk-In Shower

Leisure Room
19'-11" x 16'-4"
10'-0" to 1'-0"
Stepped Clg.

Built-In
Ent. Center
Built-In
Desk

Master Sitting
10'-0" to 10'-6"
Stepped Clg.

Lanai
32'-8" x 11'-6"
12'-0" Clg.

Nook
8'-0" x 9'-0"
10'-0" Clg.

Master Suite
18'-0" x 21'-2"
10'-0" Clg.

Pwdr.
Linen

Living Room
16'-8" x 14'-6"
12'-0" to 13'-0"
Stepped Clg.

Arch

Kitchen
16'-8" x 14'-0"
10'-0" to 10'-6"
Stepped Clg.

Master Foyer
Arch

Bar

Pantry

WIC

WIC

Bedroom 2
11'-2" x 14'-6"
10'-0" Clg.

Study
13'-0" x 15'-6"
12'-0" to 13'-0"
Stepped Clg.
Built-In

Foyer
13'-7" Clg.

Dining Room
13'-0" x 12'-6"
12'-0" to 13'-0"
Stepped Clg.

Linen

Master Bath
15'-?" x 14'-7"
10'-0" Clg.

Portico
19'-0" Clg.

Utility
x 9'-8"
10'-0" Clg.

Bath 2
Walk-In Shower

Walk-In Shower

Garage
21'-2" x 32'-4"
11'-8" Clg.

© THE SATER DESIGN
COLLECTION, INC.

Multiple windows and glass doors create a seamless connection between the indoor and outdoor living spaces.

6781 | *Rosemary Bay*

3 Bedroom

3-1/2 Bath

Living Area: **3,553** sq ft

Width: **75'0"**

Depth: **111'4"**

Exterior Walls: **8" CBS**

Foundation: slab

Price Code: **PSE5**

Southern Grace

Experience the timeless allure of Southern hospitality.

Towering stone columns, twin dormers, multi-paned windows, and a stucco and stone façade set the tone for this fashionable country estate. A second-story bowed balcony enhances the glass entryway.

Sweeping archways line the foyer that opens to the formal dining and living rooms. Pocket doors open to the private study which features a bayed window.

The leisure room boasts ample built-ins and French doors that border a wraparound rear porch. An expansive pass-thru counter opens the island kitchen to a sunny nook. An embellished hood, built-in desk and corner pantry top the kitchen's amenities.

A uniquely shaped master suite hosts a private deck, formal sitting area, large walk-in closet, two dual-sink vanities, corner whirlpool tub and a linen niche. Three bedrooms, full bath and a central utility room complete the upper level.

7038 | *Vincent*

FRONT VIEW

*The perfect balance of multi-paned windows,
French doors and stately two-story stone columns
give visual weight and drama to this timeless
country estate. The wide stone steps beautifully
connect the front lawn to the stunning front
porch, and rustic wood shutters add a classic,
handcrafted touch.*

DINING ROOM

*Located conveniently next to the kitchen and
across from the living room, the formal dining
room encourages traffic flow from both sides.
A crisp green-and-white color scheme draws
attention to the quality craftsmanship of the
woodwork in the coffered ceiling and wainscoting.*

LIVING ROOM

Careful attention to detail went into the design of this stunning and comfortable living room. Classic woodwork combines with a coffered ceiling and dramatic fireplace to create a welcoming haven.

FOYER

The gracious foyer is the perfect spot to greet family and friends. Guests can be lead into the stylish living room to enjoy cocktails and the glow of the fireplace. When dinner is ready to be served, guests step straight across the foyer into the formal dining room.

LEISURE ROOM/KITCHEN

An open, friendly layout offers natural flow between the kitchen, leisure room and breakfast nook. Defined by classic white columns, the kitchen features a butcher-block island with a prep sink for easy meal preparation and a corner walk-in pantry is conveniently placed nearby. The serving bar connects to the nook and leisure room, allowing the family "chef" to join in festive conversations. French doors connect the common area to the outdoors.

STUDY/LIBRARY

Rustic-wood bookcases fill a wall of the study adjacent to the living room. A beamed ceiling and hardwood floors add to the rich and cozy ambience. A bay window offers a charming setting for a window seat in the study, where a cup of coffee and bird watching offer a perfect break from a busy day.

MASTER BATH

Glass block encases a walk-in shower and shutters add a decorative touch to a corner-set whirlpool tub in the master bath.

MASTER BEDROOM

Windows frame the sitting area in the master suite and a handy door provides access to a private deck. A screened balcony extends the master suite outdoors and offers a calm environment for relaxing.

© THE SATER DESIGN COLLECTION, INC.

Bonus Room
12'-0" x 13'-2"

CL

Bath

Dn

REAR ELEVATION

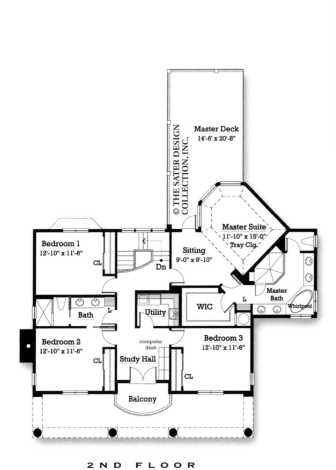

© THE SATER DESIGN COLLECTION, INC.

Master Deck
14'-6" x 20'-8"

Bedroom 1
12'-10" x 11'-6"

CL

Dn

Sitting
9'-0" x 9'-10"

Master Suite
11'-10" x 15'-0"
Tray Clg.

Bath

L

Utility

WIC

L

Master Bath

Whirlpool

Bedroom 2
12'-10" x 11'-6"

CL

computer desk

Study Hall

Bedroom 3
12'-10" x 11'-6"

CL

Balcony

2ND FLOOR

© THE SATER DESIGN COLLECTION, INC.

Garage
22'-0" x 25'-0"

Dn

Up

Porch
14'-6" x 20'-8"

Leisure Room
14'-8" x 18'-8"
Stepped Ceiling

built-ins

Nook
10'-8' x 12'-0"

Study
15'-2" x 14'-2"
Beamed Ceiling

ST

Pwdr.

desk

Kitchen
15'-8" x 15'-8"

Island

Pantry

fireplace

Up

Foyer

Dining
14'-6" x 13'-6"
Coffered Ceiling

Living
14'-6" x 16'-6"
Coffered Ceiling

Porch
42'-0" x 8'-0"

1ST FLOOR

REAR PORCH

*The perfect place to start your day, the back porch offers
a cozy spot to enjoy the morning paper and coffee.*

7038 | *Vincent*

4 Bedroom

2-1/2 Bath

1st Floor: **1,865** sq ft

2nd Floor: **1,477** sq ft

Living Area: **3,342** sq ft

Bonus Room: **282** sq ft

Width: **79'0"**

Depth: **79'2"**

Exterior Walls: **2x6**

Foundation: crawl space
or opt. basement

Price Code: **C4**

"Low Country"

An unpretentious one-story greets you with its Southern charm.

A gracious front porch invites all into this creative three-bedroom, three-bath home filled with Old-World craftsmanship, expansive windows, varied ceiling treatments and a grand verandah with an outdoor fireplace.

The spacious great room boasts built-in cabinetry and vaulted ceilings and flows into the nook and kitchen area. The central living space melds into the verandah by way of disappearing sliding glass doors, opening both rooms to an oversized outdoor living area that is anchored by a brick fireplace.

A split floor plan ensures privacy for guests and the homeowners alike. Two guest suites with full baths, walk-in closets and a private desk area flank one side of the home. Located on the opposite side, the master suite indulges with a private foyer, stepped ceiling, two walk-in closets, a luxurious bath and triple sliding doors that open to the verandah.

6780 | *Hammock Grove*

FRONT VIEW

No matter where you are, the mountains of Colorado to the cornfields of Indiana, there is something especially appealing about a front porch. The Hammock Grove combines this classic element with twin dormers, slumped arches and an abundance of windows. The result—an open invitation to stop by and say "Hello."

KITCHEN/NOOK/VERANDAH

Zero-corner sliding glass doors open to join the kitchen and verandah, where an outdoor brick fireplace warms cool evenings. The bright and airy kitchen features bead board-accented walls, decorative trim work and a large center island that provides comfortable style and modern convenience.

LIVING ROOM VIEWS

This open and free-flowing "causal zone" is design for memorable days spent with friends. An extra-wide entry to the kitchen, paired with a generous pass-thru at the bar, make entertaining easy. Quality craftsmanship is evident in the built-in cabinetry and the beamed and vaulted ceiling in the great room.

FABRIC CARE STUDIO

Designed to make your life a little easier, the Fabric Care Studio from Whirlpool™ features the Impress™ Ironing Station, DryAire™ Drying Cabinet and Duet® Fabric Care System.

Verandah
10'-0" Clg.

Outdoor Fireplace

Master Suite
13'-2" x 16'-10"
10'-0" to 10'-8"
Stepped Clg.

Built-Ins

Living Room
17'-6" x 20'-4"
10'-0" to 12'-0"
Vaulted Clg.

Nook
13'-2" x 6'-10"
10'-0" Clg.

Grille

Built-Ins

WIC

Bath 3
10'-0" Clg.

Bedroom 3
14'-0" x 12'-6"
10'-0" Clg.

WIC

Kitchen
13'-2" x 13'-5"
10'-0" Clg.

Pantry

WIC

WIC

Master Bath
10'-0" Clg.

Study
11'-4" x 16'-10"
11'-6"-12'-0"
6" Beam Clg.

Foyer
13'-4" Clg.

Dining Room
14'-0" x 12'-0"
12'-0" to 13'-0"
Stepped Clg.

Pwdr.

Bedroom 2
13'-10" x 12'-3"
10'-0" Clg.

Sink Spa

Fabric Care Studio
10'-0" Clg.
Duets W/D
Dry-Aire Cabt.

Bath 2
10'-0" Clg.

Entry
14'-0" Clg.

2-Car Garage
21'-8" x 21'-8"
10'-0" Clg.

©THE SATER DESIGN COLLECTION, INC.

Interior light spills onto the verandah through multiple sets of sliding glass doors, where an outdoor fireplace, grille and pool ensure easy entertaining.

6780 | *Hammock Grove*

3 Bedroom

3 Bath

Living Area: **2,885** sq ft

Width: **72'0"**

Depth: **80'0"**

Exterior Walls:

8" CBS OR 2X6

Foundation: slab

Price Code: **PSE5**

Country Living

Kick back and enjoy welcoming breezes and wide-open spaces.

Nostalgic design is seamlessly incorporated with state-of-the-art amenities in this coastal charmer. A spacious parlor is the perfect place to greet visitors and features expansive windows looking out on the covered porch—one like your grandparents may have had. The large and multi-functional kitchen area is open to the grand room, where a large TV niche occupies its own space beside the towering fireplace.

A generous master suite provides a quiet retreat for the homeowners, while second-floor bedrooms surrounding a computer loft give the rest of the family privacy and their own space to work and play. A connection is maintained through the hallway, which is open to the grand room via a dramatic over-look. Media built-ins abound, as the computer loft has space for high-tech equipment and shelves for books, videos and music.

6667 | *Edgewood Trail*

FRONT VIEW

A wide wraparound porch with transom windows, horizontal siding and a widow's walk make this classic exterior a look to last for generations.

KITCHEN/NOOK

Furniture-grade cabinets and wainscot detailing infuse this kitchen with old-time country flavor. Modern amenities provide contemporary convenience and granite countertops lend permanence to the entire design. Nearby, generous windows in the nook let you ease into the day with a tranquil breakfast overlooking the backyard.

GRAND ROOM/KITCHEN

A pass-thru eating bar divides the kitchen and grand room without separating the cook from the rest of the family.

GRAND ROOM

Designed for enjoying the outdoors—as well as each other's company—the grand room features a fireplace, built-in television niche and sliding glass doors opening to the back porch. Soaring windows and a two-story ceiling enhance the open, yet intimate, feeling of the common living space.

DINING ROOM

With easy access to the kitchen, the octagonal-shaped dining room is an entertainer's dream. After dinner, French doors opening to the front porch encourage guests to enjoy relaxing breezes and cocktails under the stars.

MASTER BEDROOM

A quiet haven, the private master suite enjoys a bay-window sitting nook, access to the back porch and spacious walk-in closets.

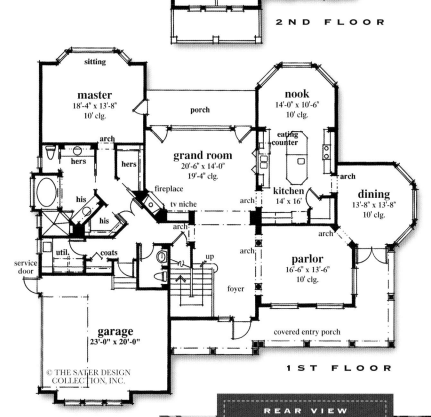

2ND FLOOR

© THE SATER DESIGN COLLECTION, INC.

br. 2
14'-0" x 16'-6"
8' clg.

open to grand room below

overlook

attic storage

down

open to below

computer loft built ins

arch

br. 3
13'-8" x 13'-8"
8' clg.

br. 4
10'-6" x 10'-6"
8' clg.

1ST FLOOR

sitting

master
18'-4" x 13'-8"
10' clg.

porch

nook
14'-0" x 10'-6"
10' clg.

arch

hers

hers

eating counter

grand room
20'-6" x 14'-0"
19'-4" clg.

fireplace

tv niche

kitchen
14' x 16'

dining
13'-8" x 13'-8"
10' clg.

arch

his

his

arch

util.

coats

service door

up

arch

arch

parlor
16'-6" x 13'-6"
10' clg.

foyer

garage
23'-0" x 20'-0"

covered entry porch

© THE SATER DESIGN COLLECTION, INC.

REAR VIEW

Outdoor spaces frame an open floor plan that takes on planned events with ease, yet also offers views of nature—and great places to relax.

6667 | Edgewood Trail

4 Bedroom

2-1/2 Bath

1st Floor: **2,241** sq ft

2nd Floor: **949** sq ft

Living Area: **3,190** sq ft

Width: **69'8"**

Depth: **61'10"**

Exterior Walls: **2x6**

Foundation: slab/ opt. basement

Price Code: **C4**

Pastoral Ranch

Spectacular porch views are 'round every corner.

Enjoy the historical charm found in the façade of this French Country Estate—stone columns, decorative shutters, multiple gables and a gracious wraparound porch. Past the foyer, the spacious interior creates an open and inviting environment. A coffered ceiling enhances the stylish study while pillars and a stepped ceiling define the formal dining room. Conveniently located nearby is the gourmet-caliber kitchen. Decorative columns line the wraparound eating bar that sits under a large loft. A two-story coffered ceiling soars over the common living space with French doors expanding the area outward.

Tucked away to the left side of the home, the private master bedroom is a quiet retreat. Sitting under a stepped ceiling, the suite features French doors that open to the back porch, a luxe bath and walk-in closet.

Two secondary bedrooms share the second floor with a generous bonus room and loft area.

7023 | *Ansel Arbor*

FRONT VIEW

From stone columns to the multiple dormers, gables and custom shutters, this home epitomizes Old-World charm. A simply striking façade, twin sets of columns line the extensive wraparound porch and multi-paned windows bring in the soft warmth of the sun.

DINING ROOM

Just off the foyer, the formal dining room enjoys an open connection with the kitchen, study and great room. Defined by pillars and a stepped ceiling, the stylish room offers a warm welcome to all who come inside.

FOYER ENTRY

The open, flowing nature of this home is readily apparent the moment guests enter through the foyer. In every direction are views of the two-story coffered ceiling in the great room, the inviting kitchen and the open loft above.

NOOK/KITCHEN

The kitchen area is filled with possibilities as guests are offered a seat at the wraparound eating bar or nearby in the comfortable nook. This entire area also opens to the wraparound porch just outside.

GREAT ROOM

Whether it's an energetic gathering of family and friends or a quiet chilly night with a blanket and a book, the great room offers comfort, convenience and warmth with handsome built-ins, a centralized fireplace and access through multiple French doors to the world outside.

REAR VIEW

Inside living space is extended outside through the extremely accessible rear wraparound porch. The home is opened up through multiple French doors from the great room and nook, but also from the master bedroom, powder room and utility rooms.

FABRIC CARE STUDIO

The Fabric Care Studio overflows with innovation and convenience. Not only does it contain the customary essentials, it is accessible from both the kitchen and the garage.

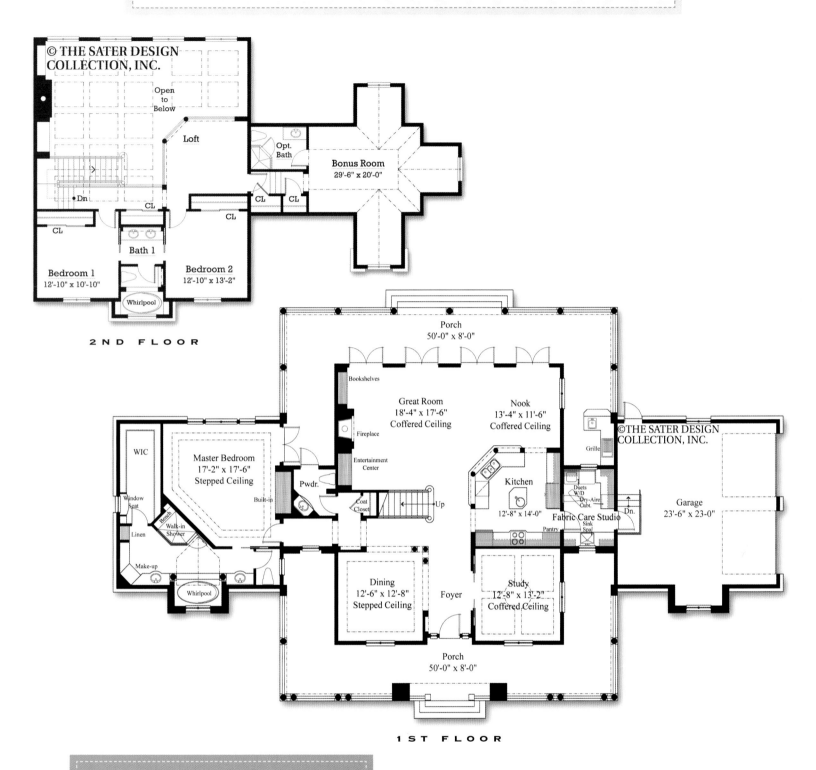

2ND FLOOR

1ST FLOOR

7023 | *Ansel Arbor*

3 Bedroom

3-1/2 Bath

Living Area: **2,889** sq ft

1st Floor: **2,151** sq ft

2nd Floor: **738** sq ft

Bonus Room: **534** sq ft

Width: **99'0"**

Depth: **56'0"**

Exterior Walls: **2x6**

Foundation: crawl space/ opt. basement

Price Code: **C3**

7065 *Lexington*

FRONT VIEW

All of the classic elements of a true country estate are found here—the appealing front porch, symmetrical dormers, multiple gables and decorative shutters. Multi-paned and transom windows lining the front porch provide views and a close connection to the outdoors.

GREAT ROOM

The substantial great room features a coffered ceiling, built-ins and open access to the kitchen and dining rooms. The great room and study share a double-sided fireplace, and both rooms boast French-door access to the rear porch.

Simply Classic

Timeless design that will last for generations to come.

The picturesque porch, lined with columns and arches, sets off decorative shutters and dormers. Inside the warm welcome continues with an open floor plan that encourages traffic flow from both wings of the home. At the center, the great room features a beamed coffered ceiling, built-ins and open access to the kitchen and dining room. A two-sided fireplace, shared with the study, adds a cozy touch to the spacious room. Three sets of French doors opening to the back porch extend the living space outside.

A split floor plan ensures privacy for the homeowner and guests alike. The master retreat features a luxe bath, specialty ceiling and French doors to the back porch. On the opposite side of the home, two guest bedrooms share a full bath. An optional bonus room offers many possibilities.

KITCHEN/DINING ROOM

A wraparound eating bar connects the great room to the kitchen. A center work island, built-in work desk and easy access to the dining room will please cooks of all levels.

MASTER BEDROOM

A relaxing retreat, the master bedroom features a bay window, French doors opening to the back porch and a stylish tray ceiling.

MASTER BATH

An indulgent walk-in shower and whirlpool-soaking tub create a spa-like atmosphere in the master bath.

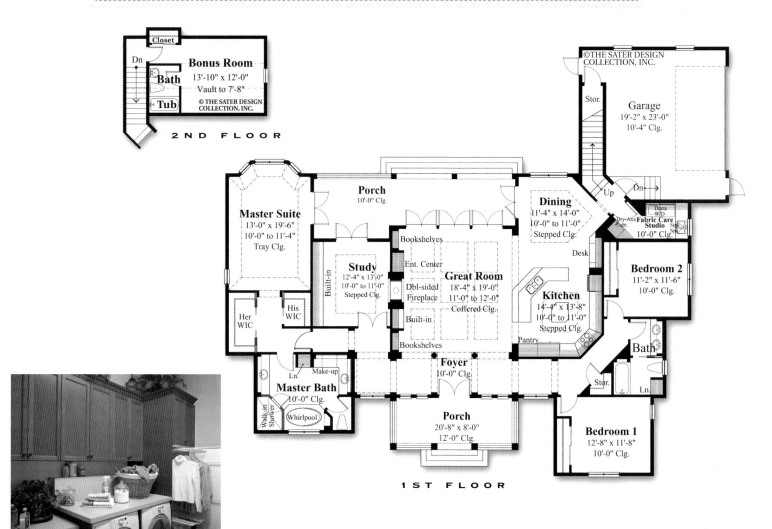

2ND FLOOR

Closet

Dn

Bath

Bonus Room
13'-10" x 12'-0"
Vault to 7'-8"
© THE SATER DESIGN
COLLECTION, INC.

Tub

©THE SATER DESIGN
COLLECTION, INC.

Garage
19'-2" x 23'-0"
10'-4" Clg.

Stor.

Up

Dn

Duct
W/D

Porch
10'-0" Clg.

Dining
11'-4" x 14'-0"
10'-0" to 11'-0"
Stepped Clg.

Dry-Aire
Cabt.

Fabric Care
Studio
10'-0" Clg.

Master Suite
13'-0" x 19'-6"
10'-0" to 11'-4"
Tray Clg.

Bookshelves

Ent. Center

Desk

Bedroom 2
11'-2" x 11'-6"
10'-0" Clg.

Built-in

Study
12'-4" x 13'-0"
10'-0" to 11'-0"
Stepped Clg.

Dbl-sided
Fireplace

Great Room
18'-4" x 19'-0"
11'-0" to 12'-0"
Coffered Clg.

Kitchen
14'-4" x 13'-8"
10'-0" to 11'-0"
Stepped Clg.

His
WIC

Her
WIC

Built-in

Bookshelves

Pantry

Bath

Ln.

Make-up

Foyer
10'-0" Clg.

Stor.

Ln.

Master Bath
10'-0" Clg.

Walk-in
Shower

Whirlpool

Porch
20'-8" x 8'-0"
12'-0" Clg.

Bedroom 1
12'-8" x 11'-8"
10'-0" Clg.

1ST FLOOR

FABRIC CARE STUDIO

Pictured above are the SinkSpa™, Duet® Fabric-Care System and DryAire™ Drying Cabinet. All are designed to make laundry fun—okay, maybe just easier to do!

REAR VIEW

7065 *Lexington*

3 Bedroom	Width: **80'6"**
2 Bath	Depth: **66'6"**
1st Floor: **2,454** sq ft	Exterior Walls: **2x6**
Living Area: **2,454** sq ft	Foundation: crawl space/slab
Bonus Room: **256** sq ft	Price Code: **C2**

Friends and family alike will enjoy the comfort of the spacious back porch—and taking a dip in the pool.

7078 | *Dune Ridge*

FRONT VIEW

Square-tapered columns, ornamental trellis brackets, exposed beams in overhanging eaves and a pleasing mix of stone and cedar shake iterate the careful attention to detail that went into the design of this Craftsman-inspired home.

DINING ROOM

Classic columns and a beamed, tray ceiling define the formal dining room. Conveniently located near the kitchen, guests will enjoy the gracious ambiance of the room.

A Crafted Design

A unique multi-generational plan that has it all.

This home celebrates the outdoors, with a floor plan that provides smart transitions between public and private realms while keeping the wide-open views in mind.

Past the gable-covered entry, the formal dining room is an open, welcoming space defined by columns and a tray ceiling.

Nearby is the home's centerpiece, the impressive great room. As grand as it is cozy, it features a fireplace, built-in cabinetry and double glass doors providing a seamless connection to the outdoors. A convenient pass-thru connects the space to the kitchen.

Tucked away from the public areas is the private master retreat. A stepped ceiling, double walk-in closets, and back-porch access—together with a lavish bath—combine to create a relaxing haven.

On the lower level, the family room is the perfect spot for entertaining with double French doors expanding the space to the backyard. Nearby, an "in-law" kitchen provides drinks and snacks for all to enjoy. Three lower-level bedrooms share a full bath and enjoy lots of natural light through multiple windows.

STUDY

Frank Lloyd Wright-inspired art-glass windows and a vaulted ceiling enhance the height and size of the study. With a spacious closet and a nearby powder bath, this room can easily convert to a guest bedroom.

FOYER

Daylight spills through the art-glass front door, transom and sidelights. An open staircase invites guests to the entertainment level below.

GREAT ROOM

The open great room flows seamlessly into the nook, kitchen and dining rooms. A vaulted coffered ceiling, double glass doors opening to the covered back porch, a fireplace and built-in cabinetry add character to the spacious room.

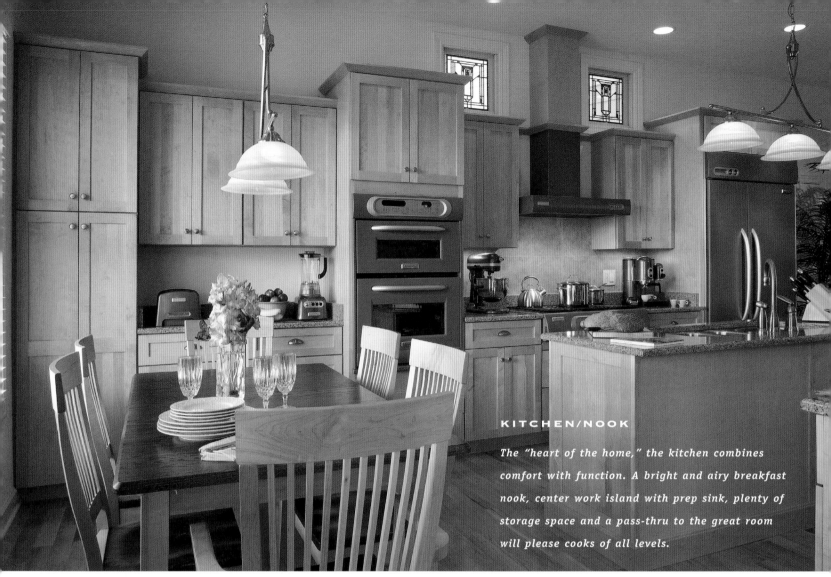

KITCHEN/NOOK

The "heart of the home," the kitchen combines comfort with function. A bright and airy breakfast nook, center work island with prep sink, plenty of storage space and a pass-thru to the great room will please cooks of all levels.

MASTER BEDROOM

The high beamed tray ceiling continues the Craftsman Style of the façade throughout the master suite. A glass door provides abundant light and private access to the outdoor covered deck.

FAMILY ROOM

A Chinese slate fireplace with raised hearth gives warmth to the lower-level family room. Beyond the French doors, summer entertainment is enhanced by an outdoor kitchen and built-in firepit that extends the season.

MASTER BATH

A WaterHaven® Custom shower with seating-for-two and art-glass windows above make a dramatic statement in the master bath.

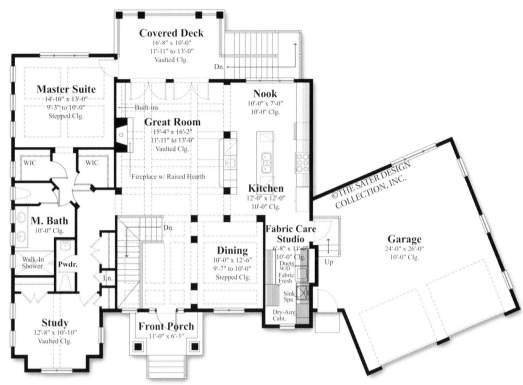

Covered Deck
16'-8" x 10'-0"
11'-11" to 13'-0"
Vaulted Clg.

Master Suite
14'-16" x 13'-0"
9'-3" to 10'-0"
Stepped Clg.

Built-ins

Nook
10'-0" x 7'-0"
10'-0" Clg.

Great Room
15'-4" x 16'-2"
11'-11" to 13'-0"
Vaulted Clg.

Fireplace w/ Raised Hearth

WIC   WIC

Kitchen
12'-0" x 12'-0"
10'-0" Clg.

©THE SATER DESIGN COLLECTION, INC.

M. Bath
10'-0" Clg.

Fabric Care Studio
6'-8" x 11'-0"
10'-0" Clg.
Duets W/D
Fabric Fresh

Garage
24'-0" x 26'-0"
10'-0" Clg.

Walk-In Shower   Pwdr.

Dining
10'-0" x 12'-6"
9'-7" to 10'-0"
Stepped Clg.

Up

Sink Spa

Dry-Aire Cabt.

Ln.

Study
12'-8" x 10'-10"
Vaulted Clg.

Front Porch
11'-0" x 6'-3"

1ST FLOOR

Deck for Outdoor Kitchen
28'-3" x 18'-8"

Heat-n-Glow Patio Campfire

Covered Patio   Up

Bedroom 3
14'-10" x 11'-2"
9'-0" Clg.

Family Room
15'-10" x 19'-2"
8'-4" to 9'-0"
Stepped Clg.

Fireplace w/ Raised Hearth

Study/Bedroom
12'-10" x 11'-6"
9'-0" Clg.

TV Nook

©THE SATER DESIGN COLLECTION, INC.

Bedroom 2
12'-2" x 13'-11"
9'-0" Clg.

Walk-In Shower

Stor.

In-Law/ Entertainment Kitchen

Bath
9'-0" Clg.

Ln.

Mech./Stor.
12'-4" x 16'-9"
9'-0" Clg.

Storage
15'-7" x 23'-0"
9'-0" Clg.

LOWER LEVEL

7078 | *Dune Ridge*

5 Bedroom
2-1/2 Bath
Lower Level: **1,193** sq ft
First Floor: **1,711** sq ft
Living Area: **2,904** sq ft

Width: **76'8"**
Depth: **52'11"**
Exterior Walls: **2x6**
Foundation: basement
Price Code: **PSE5**

Multiple windows and doors provide a connection with the outdoors while a dominant center gable brings in sunlight through square transoms. A winding staircase connects the upper and lower outdoor areas, encouraging family and guests to enjoy the upper "dining" deck as well as the lower-level outdoor kitchen and patio campfire... more S'mores, please!

New Home Trends

Outfitting your home for today's lifestyle.

Dan F. Sater II   **Mark Johnson**

Indoors and out, and even in the garage, most people want to build a home that fulfills their dreams and desires while making a statement that reflects their lifestyle. Dune Ridge (above) is a collaboration between Dan Sater of Sater Design Collection and Mark Johnson of Whirlpool Corporation that explores new trends in home design for the kitchen, outdoor kitchen, laundry space and the garage. The home is a showcase for design solutions based on Dan's inspiration, Mark's dreams, and extensive research and product development from the Whirlpool brands. We present it here for your enjoyment... perhaps you'll discover that nugget of an idea or special feature that you've dreamed about and

Trendsetting

PAGE 58

PAGE 60

ZONED KITCHEN

Extensive consumer research indicates most homeowner's lifestyle needs in the kitchen are largely unmet. They discovered consumers would prefer multiple zones in their kitchen for more than one cook, additional family members, or guests. See the research findings and design ideas on **page 58**.

FABRIC CARE STUDIO

Many consumers have moved beyond the basic laundry room with utility sink, clothes washer and dryer. Ergonomically designed appliances on pedestals, vertical storage towers with retractable hanging rods, integrated folding/work surfaces, and even in-home appliances for removing odors and wrinkles are all available. See what a Fabric Care Studio can encompass on **page 60**.

PAGE 64

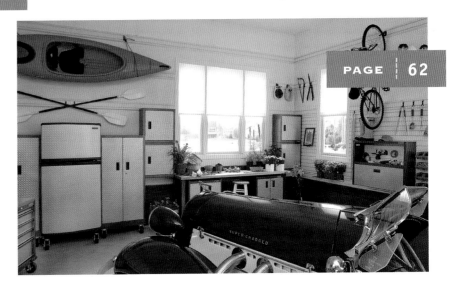

PAGE 62

OUTDOOR ENTERTAINING

One of the hottest new home trends is outdoor entertaining and cooking... and it's much bigger than an hibatchi. An outdoor room with a fully functional kitchen for grilling meats, sautéing mushrooms, preparing drinks, making ice, and storing condiments is the order of the day. See whether a built-in or freestanding outdoor kitchen is better suited for your needs on **page 64**.

MODULAR WORKSHOP & STORAGE FOR THE GARAGE

When it comes to design, the garage is typically overlooked and too often an embarrassment to the homeowner, but it doesn't have to be that way. The advent of integrated modular worksurfaces, handsome upscale storage components, and appliances designed for outdoor temperatures is changing the way garages are designed. Turn to **page 62**.

Kitchen Zone Design

With the rise of open-plan kitchens, casual dining and entertaining, multiple cooks working in the same area, and those who aspire to culinary perfection, the basic kitchen work triangle is no longer adequate. An ideal solution for a new kitchen incorporates multiple, independent work zones that are appointed to meet your personal needs and design preferences.

The *Dune Ridge* (pages 50-55) plan shows how several zones can be incorporated into a kitchen to reflect a family's particular lifestyle. It also demonstrates how task areas are being decentralized throughout the home to accommodate greater flexibility for extended family and entertaining guests.

PREP ZONE

At *Dune Ridge*, a Prep Zone is where the kids make waffles on Saturday mornings. When entertaining, the space becomes a Serving/Staging Zone for informal meals and easy cleanup.

"IN-LAW"/ENTERTAINMENT KITCHEN

Dune Ridge is designed for multi-generational use. The lower level is easily convertible from In-Law Suite, to Entertainment Space, to "Teen Haven". The galley-style kitchenette supports light cooking and clean-up with a prep sink, built-in speed-cook oven, and dishwasher drawers. An undercounter beverage center and built-in ice maker create an entertaining zone.

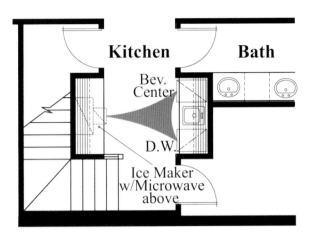

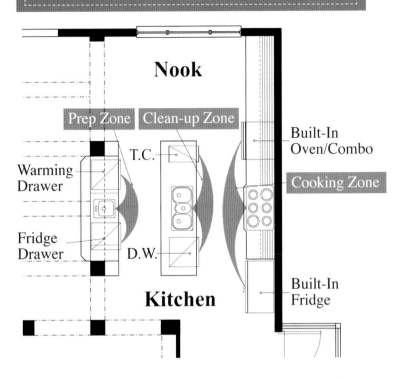

A remote kitchenette makes cooking and entertaining more convenient than a single kitchen. The *Dune Ridge* owners love entertaining upstairs with family friends while letting the kids take over the downstairs kitchenette for their own party. When grandma and grandpa visit, the kitchenette is right outside the guest room for their convenience and a little privacy.

The main kitchen at *Dune Ridge* incorporates three zones; Cooking, Clean-up and Prep Zone. The Cooking Zone is comprised of a combination convection oven with microwave above, high-performance cooktop with vent hood above, and a built-in refrigerator/freezer. The Clean-up zone includes a triple sink w/disposal, tall-tub dishwasher and trash compactor. The Prep Zone in the second island easily converts to a Serving or Staging Zone as needed.

Online Survey

If you're curious about kitchen zones, please use the free online tool at **www.kitchensforcooks.ca** and discover your kitchen lifestyle preferences. You'll see solutions tailored to your needs that can be adapted to any size home, including the following:

Cooking Zone – The starting point for every kitchen. This zone encompasses the cooktop, oven, refrigerator and perhaps a sink, and is designed to address basic cooking needs.

Clean-up Zone – This area includes the primary sink, at least one dishwasher, a trash compactor, a recycling bin, and staging area for dishes.

Prep Zone – A zone dedicated to preparation might have an additional sink and storage for items like cutting boards. A separate undercounter refrigerator or refrigerator drawer keeps ingredients fresh and close at hand.

Entertaining Zone – A dedicated area for entertaining is ideal for the social cook. Keeping guests out of harm's way and glasses full by using an undercounter beverage center and ice maker keeps entertaining on track. Adding a small-capacity dishwasher can take care of glassware at point-of-use.

Baking Zone – Double convection ovens, a lowered counter surface for rolling dough, and integrated cooling racks will help any baking enthusiast create their masterpieces undisturbed.

Kids Zone – Whether your kids are involved in the cooking process or you're just keeping them at arm's length, safety is a major concern in the kitchen. A dedicated area where they can get snacks/beverages and stay occupied while you work can be a great solution for families with young ones.

Staging/Serving Zone – Hosting a big group? The Staging Zone is an area to keep items warm, ice down drinks, and add the final touches to your culinary masterpiece. It doubles as a Serving Zone and can be equipped with a warming drawer, prep sink, and ice maker.

www.kitchenaid.com

Fabric Care Studio

Reinventing the Laundry Room

Fabric care in *Dune Ridge* is a breeze. With natural daylight and ventilation, a front-loading energy-efficient clothes washer and dryer on pedestals for easy access, lot's of storage and pantry space, a folding area and high-performance laundry sink—what more could a homeowner want?

Whether you're a family of seven or a single individual, everyone has to do laundry. Why not save time and effort by designing a space in your home that makes the task more efficient? That's the concept behind the Whirlpool Fabric Care Studio. Whether your washer and dryer priority is high-capacity, stackable units for space savings, controls at your preferred height, or making a color statement, there are options to fit your needs. Likewise, there are new Fabric Care accessories like matching storage towers, integrated worksurfaces, and appliance pedestals. Start with a washer and dryer and start building a solution around that. If you need more folding room in the space, a worksurface or pull-out shelf might be the answer. To avoid unnecessary bending which can cause fatigue, choose a pedestal to bring the washer and dryer to a better working height. Design your cabinetry to incorporate stow-away hampers in appropriate locations, a hanging area and a space for a Fabric Freshener.

www.whirlpool.com

EASIER ON CLOTHES THAN DRY CLEANING

Fabric Freshener is a new-to-the-world appliance that removes odors and wrinkles from clothing in just 30 minutes. It's portable, lightweight, uses no chemicals (just distilled water), and is only 10" tall when closed for easy storage.

FABRIC CARE STUDIO

Fabric Care Studio

Duet W/D
Fabric Fresh
Sink Spa
Dry-Aire Cabt.
Up

In contrast to many laundry rooms, the Fabric Care Studio at *Dune Ridge* is enlarged to include a window, more cabinetry, and upscale appliances, transforming the space into a welcoming destination.

Modular Workshop
and Storage Systems

Rethinking the garage

The *Dune Ridge* garage doubles as a home workshop where Gladiator GarageWorks components can be configured for the ultimate experience in garage utility, beauty, and organization. Wall cabinets, hooks and accessories can be easily moved on either the GearWall® Panels or GearTrack™ Channels for infinite customization. Freestanding and movable work benches with durable work surfaces make this garage a delight for tackling any project. GearBox Lockers, Cabinets, and Convertible Refrigerator/Freezers are the perfect solution for the sports enthusiast, avid gardener, or weekend mechanic who likes to spend hours in the garage.

Garages have become more than just a place to store the car. Historically they have been places of inspiration for great names such as Henry Ford, Walt Disney, and Steve

Jobs. Today they serve as playgrounds for everyone from gardeners to car enthusiasts. The key to any of these endeavors is space—the space that you get by moving things off the floor and onto the walls.

Garage organization with the Gladiator GarageWorks system not only helps to achieve this goal, but the modularity of the system allows it to grow and adapt with your needs. Durable components made of powdercoated steel and work surfaces made of butcher-block solid maple are as functional as they are stylish.

The addition of garage-tough Gladiator GarageWorks appliances provides added capacity to store either refrigerated or frozen foods, especially during the holiday season when space is at a premium. So open the garage door and discover a new definition for "curb appeal." **www.gladiatorgw.com**

FLEXIBILITY IN THE GARAGE

GearBox and GearDrawer components on heavy-duty casters can be used independently or joined with a VersaTop™ to create a movable workbench/storage/tool center.

GARAGE PLAN

8' Workbench

Wall Cabinet

Tall Cabinet

Freezerator

Portable
Work Island

Fold Down
Work Surface

Up

**Gladiator
Garageworks
Garage**

GearTrack
& Accessories

GearWall
& Accessories

WALL SYSTEMS AND COMPONENTS

A new fold-down stainless-steel work surface with storage shelves is the latest Gladiator GarageWorks component. GearWall® Panels and GearTrack™ Channels support the system components and can be used independently or combined as shown here for *Dune Ridge*.

Extra depth at the back of the *Dune Ridge* garage allows easy access to the workbench, modular cabinets, and Convertible Refrigerator/Freezer. Large windows provide views, plenty of natural light and ventilation, and a feeling of warmth to the garage.

BUILT-IN KITCHEN

A built-in outdoor kitchen is the ultimate commitment to cooking in the open air and under the stars. Food prepared on an outdoor grille just seems to taste better. What's more, a built-in kitchen becomes an architectural element of the home's design—an "outdoor room" in the back yard—and acts as an extension of the home.

FREE-STANDING KITCHEN

A free-standing outdoor kitchen offers infinite flexibility in layout and staging for any number of guests. If you live in a climate zone with harsh winters, you have the option of moving the appliances inside for the winter, or if you relocate, taking the appliances along. You can extend the outdoor season by adding a fire pit or outdoor fireplace.

Contributors

Dan F. Sater, II and Whirlpool Corporation would like to thank the following companies for their involvement in making the award-winning Dune Ridge home a reality.

Andersen Windows - Frank Lloyd Wright Series

Azek - Exterior Trimboards

Cambria - Natural Quartz Surfaces

Delta Faucets - Brizo & Michael Graves Collections

Leviton - Acenti Collection - Lighting Controls

Hearth & Home - Heat & Glo Fireplaces

Kohler - Bathroom Fixtures

Nailite International - RoughSawn Cedar Siding

Omega Cabinetry - Dynasty Collection

Walpole Woodworkers - Freeport Collection

Shamrock Construction - Home Builder

Classic Country

How does a classic...become a classic? A sense of style is certainly important. A well-known standard of refinement and elegance is also essential. But we like to think that classics are formed by endurance. By time. You do not witness them being produced or fabricated — true classics evolve and grow, building significance and impact across generations. That's why these Classic Country designs have been created with the highest, most established, standards of style. You need only to glance through the homes on the pages that follow to understand what truly defines a classic. The simple, harmonious lines of wide, expansive porches, gables and traditional dormers; the quiet beauty of flowing, open floor plans; strong, elegant columns and impressive built-in cabinetry; wide-open gourmet kitchens and luxuriant, secluded master suites — these are the elements that have endured over time.

© THE SATER DESIGN COLLECTION, INC.

REAR ELEVATION

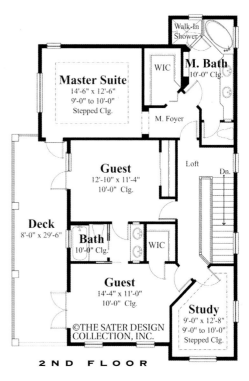

CABRINI | 6516

A wraparound portico, vented gables and louvered shutters garner attention from those who pass by the Cabrini. Inside, columns and specialty ceilings define the dining and great rooms while multiple sets of French doors open the common living space to the outdoors. Nearby, the kitchen features a convenient pass-thru and center work island. On the upper level, the master suite and secondary bedrooms enjoy privacy and access to the deck.

3 Bedroom / **2-1/2** Bath

1st Floor: **1,085** sq ft

2nd Floor: **1,093** sq ft

Living Area: **2,178** sq ft

Width: **32'8"**

Depth: **72'0"**

Exterior Walls: **2x6**

Foundation: slab

Price Code: **C2**

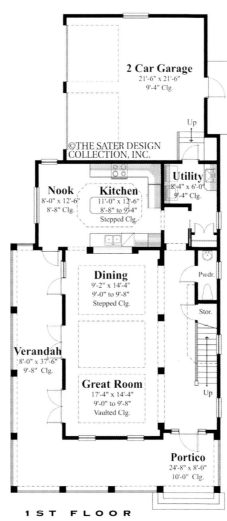

1ST FLOOR

2 Car Garage
21'-6" x 21'-6"
9'-4" Clg.

©THE SATER DESIGN COLLECTION, INC.

Up

Utility
8'-4" x 6'-0"
9'-4" Clg.

Nook
8'-0" x 12'-6"
8'-8" Clg.

Kitchen
11'-0" x 12'-6"
8'-8" to 9'-4"
Stepped Clg.

Dining
9'-2" x 14'-4"
9'-0" to 9'-8"
Stepped Clg.

Pwdr.

Stor.

Verandah
8'-0" x 37'-6"
9'-8" Clg.

Great Room
17'-4" x 14'-4"
9'-0" to 9'-8"
Vaulted Clg.

Up

Portico
24'-8" x 8'-0"
10'-0" Clg.

2ND FLOOR

Walk-In Shower

WIC

M. Bath
10'-0" Clg.

Master Suite
14'-6" x 12'-6"
9'-0" to 10'-0"
Stepped Clg.

M. Foyer

Guest
12'-10" x 11'-4"
10'-0" Clg.

Loft

Dn.

Deck
8'-0" x 29'-6"

Bath
10'-0" Clg.

WIC

Guest
14'-4" x 11'-0"
10'-0" Clg.

Study
9'-0" x 12'-8"
9'-0" to 10'-0"
Stepped Clg.

©THE SATER DESIGN COLLECTION, INC.

© THE SATER DESIGN COLLECTION, INC.

REAR VIEW

6755 | CARLILE BAY

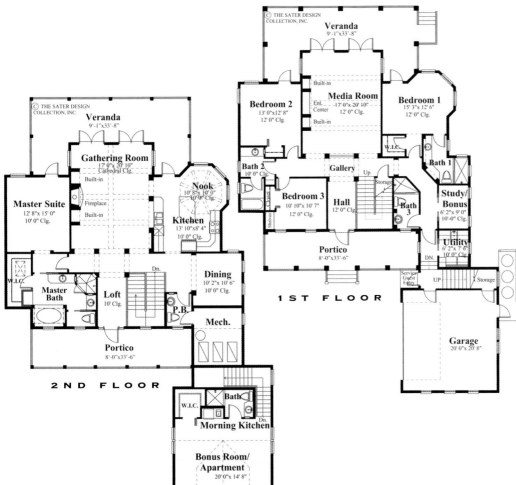

Veranda
9'-1"x33'-8"

Media Room
17'0"x20'40"
12' 0" Clg.

Bedroom 2
13'0"x12'8"
12'0" Clg

Bedroom 1
15'3"x12'6"
12'0" Clg

Ent. Center

Built-in

Built-in

Bath 2
10'0" Clg.

W.I.C.

Bath 1

Gallery

Up

Storage

Bedroom 3
10'10"x10'7"
12'0" Clg.

Hall
12'0" Clg.

Study/ Bonus
6'2"x 9'0"
10'-0" Clg.

Bath 3

Utility
6'2"x 7'6"
10'0" Clg.

Portico
8'-0"x33'-6"

Service Guest Entry

UP

Storage

Dn.

1ST FLOOR

Garage
20'0"x 20'8"

Veranda
9'-1"x33'-8"

Gathering Room
17'0"x 20'10"
Cathedral Clg.

Built-in

Built-in

Fireplace

Nook
10'8"x 10'0"
10'0" Clg.

Kitchen
13'10"x8'4"
10'0" Clg.

Master Suite
12'8"x 15'0"
10'0" Clg.

W.I.C.

Master Bath

Loft
10' Clg.

P.B.

Dn.

Dining
10'2"x 10'6"
10'0" Clg.

Mech.

Portico
8'-0"x33'-6"

2ND FLOOR

Bath

W.I.C.

Dn.

Morning Kitchen

Bonus Room/ Apartment
20'0"x 14'8"

Balcony

Wide verandas and a double portico enrich the sidewalk presentation of Carlile Bay. The entry hall leads past the centered gallery, defined by columns and arches, to the media room, equipped with a built-in entertainment center and cabinetry. A flex room connects the service entry and utility zone with an angled hall and luxe bedroom suite. On the upper level, French doors open the gathering room to the veranda.

5 Bedroom / **5-1/2** Bath

1st Floor: **1,766** sq ft

2nd Floor: **1,582** sq ft

Living Area: **3,348** sq ft

Bonus Room: **434** sq ft

Width: **56'0"**

Depth: **80'0"**

Exterior Walls: **2x6**

Foundation: crawl space

Price Code: **C4**

REAR ELEVATION

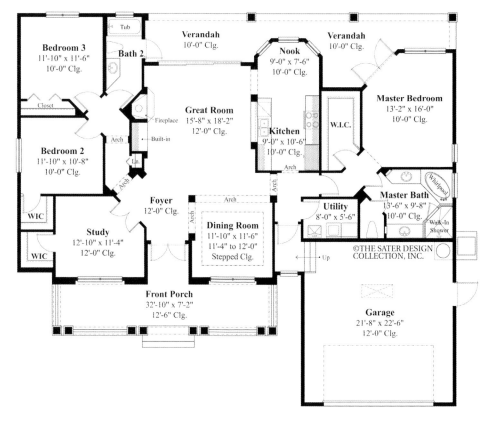

MAYWOOD | 6776

Find classic charm in each multi-pane window, the double columns, and in the multiple dormers of the façade. Maywood is an especially open floor plan with large dining, kitchen and great rooms divided by columns and arches. Extending the living space outside, retreating glass doors open the great room to the veranda. This split-floor plan affords easy privacy for the master suite and two secondary bedrooms.

3 Bedroom / **2** Bath

Living Area: **1,911** sq ft

Width: **64'0"**

Depth: **55'0"**

Exterior Walls: **2x6**

Foundation: crawl space

Price Code: **C1**

© THE SATER DESIGN COLLECTION, INC.

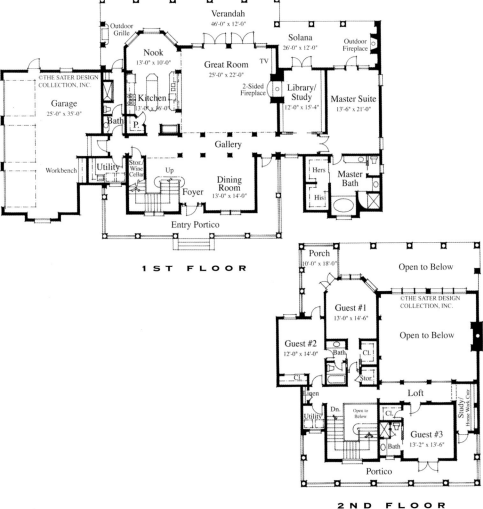

1ST FLOOR

- Outdoor Grille
- Verandah 46'-0" x 12'-0"
- Nook 13'-0" x 10'-0"
- Solana 26'-0" x 12'-0"
- Outdoor Fireplace
- ©THE SATER DESIGN COLLECTION, INC.
- Great Room 25'-0" x 22'-0" TV
- Kitchen 13'-4" x 16'-0"
- 2-Sided Fireplace
- Library/ Study 12'-0" x 15'-4"
- Master Suite 13'-6" x 21'-0"
- Garage 25'-0" x 35'-0"
- Bath
- P.
- Gallery
- Workbench
- Utility
- Stor./ Wine Cellar
- Up
- Foyer
- Dining Room 13'-0" x 14'-0"
- Hers
- His
- Master Bath
- Entry Portico

2ND FLOOR

- Porch 10'-0" x 18'-0"
- Guest #1 13'-0" x 14'-6"
- Open to Below
- ©THE SATER DESIGN COLLECTION, INC.
- Open to Below
- Guest #2 12'-0" x 14'-0"
- Bath
- Cl.
- Linen
- Utility
- Dn.
- Open to Below
- Loft
- Study/ House Work Cntr
- Cl.
- Guest #3 13'-2" x 13'-6"
- Bath
- Stor.
- Portico

REAR ELEVATION

6782 | ANNA BELLE

Two-story columns support the front porch and roof above, creating shade and security for this plantation-inspired home. A view-oriented design, the plan allows spectacular vistas, even from the front door. Columns and French doors define the great room, which hosts a two-sided fireplace and built-in cabinetry. To the right of the plan, the study maintains privacy for the master wing. Located on the second level, guest bedrooms enjoy porch access.

4 Bedroom / **4** Bath

1st Floor: **2,701** sq ft

2nd Floor: **1,390** sq ft

Living Area: **4,091** sq ft

Width: **98'0"**

Depth: **60'0"**

Exterior Walls: **2x6**

Foundation: crawl space

Price Code: **L2**

REAR ELEVATION

© THE SATER DESIGN COLLECTION, INC.

PALMA RIOS | 6863

A vented central dormer tops a series of multi-level rooflines — supported by a column-lined entry porch. Inside, an open arrangement of the formal rooms creates an inviting atmosphere. Retreating glass doors allow the formal living and dining spaces to extend to the veranda. A convenient eating bar connects the kitchen to the leisure and dining rooms. Upstairs, the master suite adjoins a spare room that could serve as a study, and leads out to a rear deck.

4 Bedroom / **2-1/2** Bath

1st Floor: **1,562** sq ft

2nd Floor: **1,281** sq ft

Living Area: **2,843** sq ft

Width: **41'6"**

Depth: **67'0"**

Exterior Walls: **2x6**

Foundation: slab

Price Code: **C3**

1ST FLOOR

Leisure Room
15'-0" x 17'-2"
10'-0" to 11'-0"
Step Clg.

© THE SATER DESIGN COLLECTION, INC.

Dining
17'-0" x 12'-6"
10'-0" Clg.

Veranda
10'-10" x 11'-8"
9'-4" Clg.

Kitchen
14'-8" x 16'-6"
10'-0".

Pantry

Storage

Living Room
15'-6" x 18'-8"
10'-0"

Desk

Pwdr.

Fireplace

Up

Utility

Garage
21'-0" x 21'-6"
10'-4" Clg.

Foyer
5'-6" x 10'-6"
10'-0"

Study
11'-8" x 11'-2"
10'-0" to 11'-0"
Step Clg.

Entry/Porch

2ND FLOOR

© THE SATER DESIGN COLLECTION, INC.

Tub

Walk-in Shower

Master Bedroom
17'-2" x 12'-6"
8'-0" to 9'-0" Tray Clg.

Master Porch
10'-10" x 11'-8"
8'-0" Clg.

Master Bath

W.I.C.

Open to Below
18'-0" Beamed Clg.

Dn.

Overlook

Closet

Closet

Bedroom 1
10'-2" x 12'-0"
8'-0" Clg.

Bath

Overlook

Open to Below

Bedroom 3
11'-8" x 10'-6"
8'-0" Clg.

Bedroom 2
10'-6" x 11'-8"
8'-0" Clg.

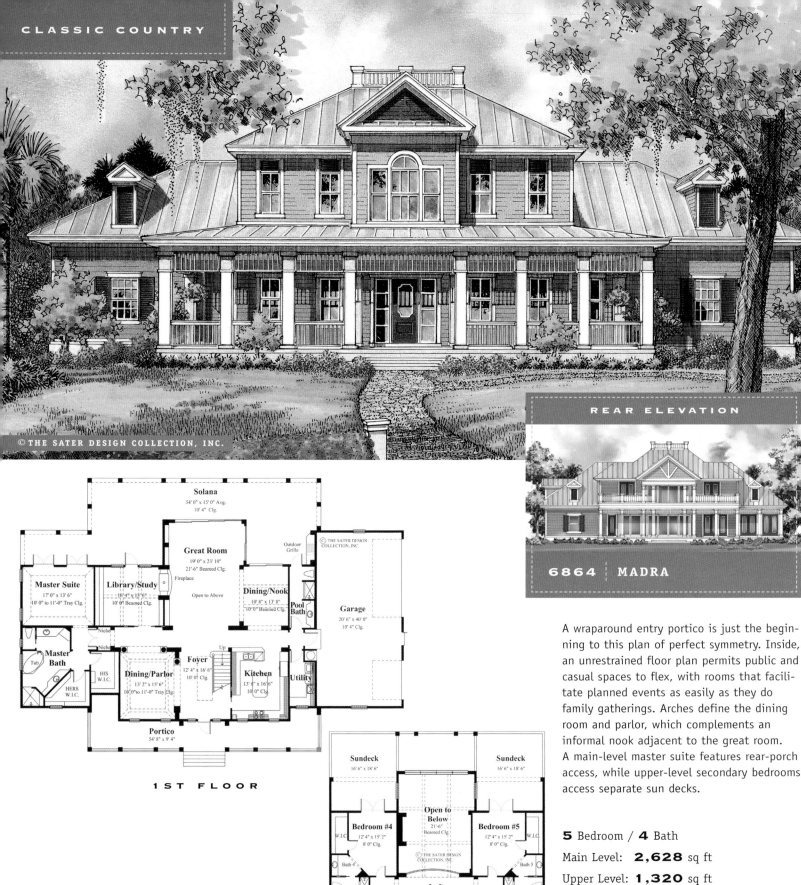

© THE SATER DESIGN COLLECTION, INC.

REAR ELEVATION

6864 | MADRA

1ST FLOOR

- Solana — 54' 0" x 15' 0" Avg. — 10' 4" Clg.
- Great Room — 19' 0" x 23' 10" — 21'-6" Beamed Clg. — Open to Above
- Library/Study — 15' 4" x 13' 6" — 10' 0" Beamed Clg.
- Master Suite — 17' 0" x 13' 6" — 10' 0" to 11'-0" Tray Clg.
- Master Bath
- HERS W.I.C.
- HIS W.I.C.
- Niche
- Dining/Nook — 10' 8" x 13' 8" — 10' 0" Beamed Clg.
- Outdoor Grille
- Pool Bath
- Garage — 20' 6" x 40' 0" — 10' 4" Clg.
- Foyer — 12' 4" x 16' 6" — 10' 0" Clg.
- Dining/Parlor — 13' 2" x 15' 6" — 10' 0" to 11'-0" Tray Clg.
- Kitchen — 13' 6" x 16' 6" — 10' 0" Clg.
- Utility
- Up
- Fireplace
- Portico — 54' 8" x 9' 4"

© THE SATER DESIGN COLLECTION, INC.

2ND FLOOR

- Sundeck — 16' 6" x 18' 6"
- Sundeck — 16' 6" x 18' 6"
- Bedroom #4 — 12' 4" x 15' 2" — 8' 0" Clg.
- Bedroom #5 — 12' 4" x 15' 2" — 8' 0" Clg.
- Open to Below — 21'-6" Beamed Clg.
- W.I.C.
- Bath 4
- Bath 5
- Bath 2
- Bath 3
- Loft
- Dn.
- Bedroom #2 — 13' 6" x 12' 2" — 8' 0" Clg.
- Bedroom #3 — 13' 6" x 12' 2" — 8' 0" Clg.

© THE SATER DESIGN COLLECTION, INC.

A wraparound entry portico is just the beginning to this plan of perfect symmetry. Inside, an unrestrained floor plan permits public and casual spaces to flex, with rooms that facilitate planned events as easily as they do family gatherings. Arches define the dining room and parlor, which complements an informal nook adjacent to the great room. A main-level master suite features rear-porch access, while upper-level secondary bedrooms access separate sun decks.

5 Bedroom / **4** Bath

Main Level: **2,628** sq ft

Upper Level: **1,320** sq ft

Living Area: **3,948** sq ft

Width: **92'0"**

Depth: **63'0"**

Exterior Walls: **2x6**

Foundation: slab or crawl space

Price Code: **L2**

© THE SATER DESIGN COLLECTION, INC.

REAR ELEVATION

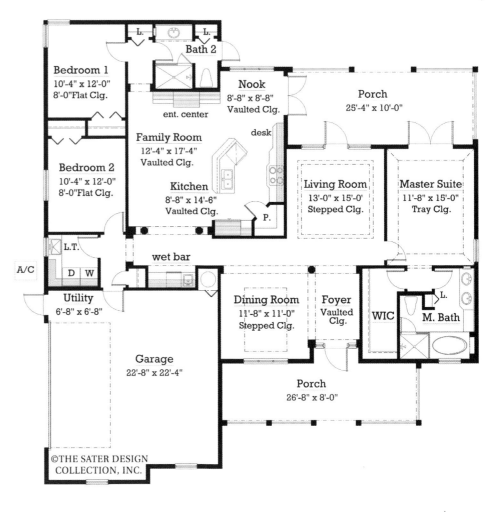

RIVERWOOD | 7001

From the multiple gables to the transom windows with louvered shutters, Riverwood embodies traditional elegance. This roomy, private floor plan features an open kitchen with large pantry and nook, and the spacious family room is flanked by a wet bar and built-in entertainment center. A huge walk-in closet and master bath, along with French doors to the back porch, make for an impressive and private master suite.

3 Bedroom / **2** Bath

Living Area: **1,848** sq ft

Width: **58'0"**

Depth: **59'6"**

Exterior Walls: **2x6**

Foundation: crawl space

Price Code: **C1**

Bedroom 1
10'-4" x 12'-0"
8'-0"Flat Clg.

Bath 2

Nook
8'-8" x 8'-8"
Vaulted Clg.

Porch
25'-4" x 10'-0"

ent. center

Bedroom 2
10'-4" x 12'-0"
8'-0"Flat Clg.

Family Room
12'-4" x 17'-4"
Vaulted Clg.

desk

Kitchen
8'-8" x 14'-6"
Vaulted Clg.

Living Room
13'-0" x 15'-0"
Stepped Clg.

Master Suite
11'-8" x 15'-0"
Tray Clg.

A/C

L.T.

D W

wet bar

Utility
6'-8" x 6'-8"

Dining Room
11'-8" x 11'-0"
Stepped Clg.

Foyer
Vaulted Clg.

WIC

M. Bath

Garage
22'-8" x 22'-4"

Porch
26'-8" x 8'-0"

©THE SATER DESIGN
COLLECTION, INC.

© THE SATER DESIGN COLLECTION, INC.

7004 | ASHTON OAKS

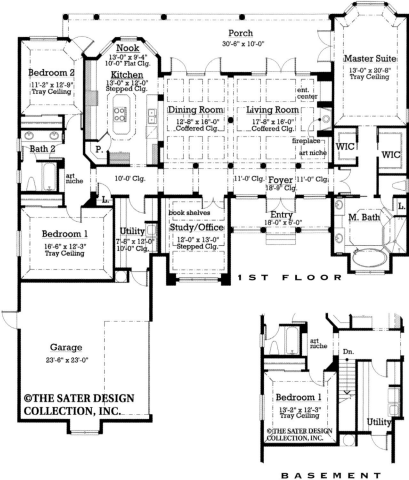

The statley dormer-topped porch entry rests between a pair of classic gables. Inside, more columns and coffered ceilings provide understated elegance to the living and dining rooms. With its handy pass-thru to the dining room, the kitchen also features a walk-in pantry and spacious nook. Enjoy the view through a wall of windows from the office or exit the huge master suite through French doors.

3 Bedroom / **2** Bath

Living Area: **2,487** sq ft

Width: **70'0"**

Depth: **72'0"**

Exterior Walls: **2x6**

Foundation: slab/opt. basement

Price Code: **C2**

© THE SATER DESIGN COLLECTION, INC.

REAR ELEVATION

LANCHESTER | 7007

A trio of gable-topped dormers dominate an elegant wraparound porch. The plan's centerpiece — an impressive, open great room — features a fireplace, built-in cabinetry and French doors under a vaulted beamed ceiling. A pair of spare bedrooms feature built-in desks and walk-in closets. A stepped ceiling, walk-in closets and a lavish bath complement the master suite.

3 Bedroom / **3** Bath

1st Floor: **1,716** sq ft

2nd Floor: **618** sq ft

Living Area: **2,334** sq ft

Width: **47'0"**

Depth: **50'0"**

Exterior Walls: **2x6**

Foundation: crawl space/ opt. basement

Price Code: **C2**

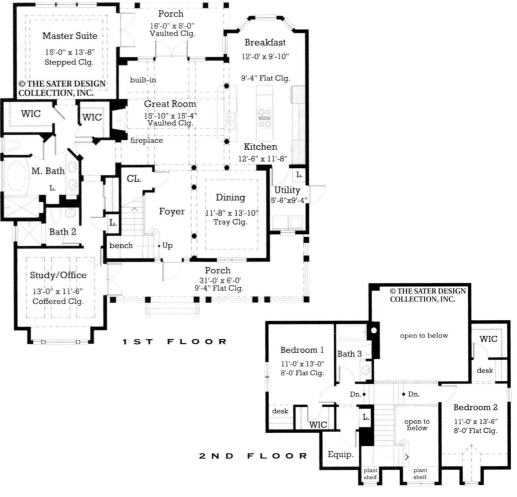

© THE SATER DESIGN COLLECTION, INC.

Master Suite
15'-0" x 13'-8"
Stepped Clg.

Porch
16'-0" x 8'-0"
Vaulted Clg.

Breakfast
12'-0" x 9'-10"
9'-4" Flat Clg.

built-in

WIC   WIC

Great Room
15'-10" x 15'-4"
Vaulted Clg.

Kitchen
12'-6" x 11'-8"

M. Bath
L.

fireplace

CL.

Utility
5'-6"x9'-4"

L.

Foyer

Dining
11'-8" x 13'-10"
Tray Clg.

L.

Bath 2

bench   • Up

Study/Office
13'-0" x 11'-6"
Coffered Clg.

Porch
31'-0" x 6'-0"
9'-4" Flat Clg.

1ST FLOOR

© THE SATER DESIGN COLLECTION, INC.

open to below

Bedroom 1
11'-0' x 13'-0"
8'-0' Flat Clg.

Bath 3

WIC

desk

desk

Dn.   • Dn.

WIC

Bedroom 2
11'-0' x 13'-6"
8'-0' Flat Clg.

L.

open to below

2ND FLOOR

Equip.

plant shelf   plant shelf

© THE SATER DESIGN COLLECTION, INC.

7010 | DELMARE

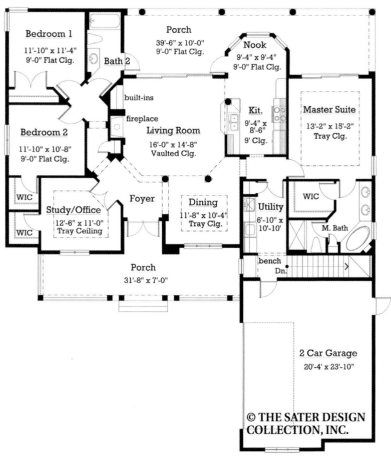

Bedroom 1
11'-10" x 11'-4"
9'-0" Flat Clg.

Bath 2

Porch
39'-6" x 10'-0"
9'-0" Flat Clg.

Nook
9'-4" x 9'-4"
9'-0" Flat Clg.

built-ins

Master Suite
13'-2" x 15'-2"
Tray Clg.

fireplace

Living Room
16'-0" x 14'-8"
Vaulted Clg.

Kit.
9'-4" x 8'-6"
9' Clg.

Bedroom 2
11'-10" x 10'-8"
9'-0" Flat Clg.

WIC

Foyer

Dining
11'-8" x 10'-4"
Tray Clg.

Utility
6'-10" x 10'-10'

WIC

Study/Office
12'-6" x 11'-0"
Tray Ceiling

WIC

M. Bath

bench
Dn.

Porch
31'-8" x 7'-0"

2 Car Garage
20'-4' x 23'-10"

© THE SATER DESIGN
COLLECTION, INC.

Classic beauty surrounds Delmare — from its multiple gables and dormer windows to the deep covered front and rear porches. This open, airy plan features a vaulted ceiling in the living room as well as built-in cabinetry, a fireplace and retreating glass doors. The breakfast nook and master suite both open up to the back porch, and the plan's study could easily function as a fourth bedroom.

3 Bedroom / **2** Bath

Living Area: **1,822** sq ft

Width: **58'4"**

Depth: **66'8"**

Exterior Walls: **2x6**

Foundation: basement

Price Code: **C1**

© THE SATER DESIGN COLLECTION, INC.

REAR ELEVATION

FOX HOLLOW | 7013

From the sunburst transom windows to the gabled dormers and covered front porch, Fox Hollow makes for a bright, welcoming home. This open, expansive floor plan offers elegant columns, built-in cabinetry, kitchen work island and pass-thru — even a bonus room with separate entry. A secluded master suite, pampering master bath and multiple sets of French doors throughout add to the appeal.

3 Bedroom / **4-1/2** Bath

1st Floor: **1,842** sq ft

2nd Floor: **739** sq ft

Living Area: **2,581** sq ft

Bonus Room: **379** sq ft

Width: **79'0"**

Depth: **50'0"**

Exterior Walls: **2x6**

Foundation: crawl space/opt. basement

Price Code: **C3**

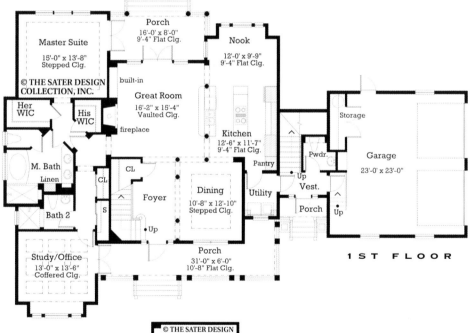

© THE SATER DESIGN COLLECTION, INC.

Master Suite
15'-0" x 13'-8"
Stepped Clg.

Porch
16'-0" x 8'-0"
9'-4" Flat Clg.

Nook
12'-0" x 9'-9"
9'-4" Flat Clg.

built-in

Her WIC

His WIC

Great Room
16'-2" x 15'-4"
Vaulted Clg.

fireplace

Kitchen
12'-6" x 11'-7"
9'-4" Flat Clg.

Storage

Garage
23'-0" x 23'-0"

M. Bath

Linen

Pantry

Pwdr.

Up

Vest.

CL

CL

Foyer

Dining
10'-8" x 12'-10"
Stepped Clg.

Utility

Up

Porch

Bath 2

S

Up

Study/Office
13'-0" x 13'-6"
Coffered Clg.

Porch
31'-0" x 6'-0"
10'-8" Flat Clg.

1ST FLOOR

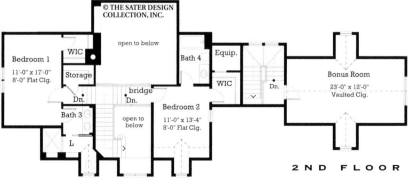

© THE SATER DESIGN COLLECTION, INC.

Bedroom 1
11'-0" x 17'-0"
8'-0" Flat Clg.

WIC

open to below

Bath 4

Equip.

Storage

WIC

Bonus Room
23'-0" x 12'-0"
Vaulted Clg.

Dn.

bridge

Dn.

Dn.

Bath 3

open to below

Bedroom 2
11'-0" x 13'-4"
8'-0" Flat Clg.

L

2ND FLOOR

© THE SATER DESIGN COLLECTION, INC.

7016 | KENTON FARMS

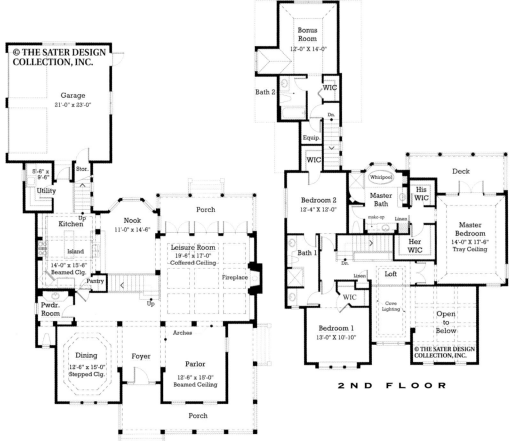

© THE SATER DESIGN COLLECTION, INC.

Garage
21'-0" x 23'-0"

5'-6" x 9'-6" Stor.

Utility

Up

Kitchen

Island
14'-0" x 15'-6"
Beamed Clg.

Nook
11'-0" x 14'-6"

Pantry

Porch

Leisure Room
19'-6" x 17'-0"
Coffered Ceiling

Fireplace

Pwdr. Room

Up

Arches

Dining
12'-6" x 15'-0"
Stepped Clg.

Foyer

Parlor
12'-6" x 15'-0"
Beamed Ceiling

Porch

1ST FLOOR

Bonus Room
12'-0" X 14'-0"

Bath 2   WIC

Dn.

Equip.

WIC

Whirlpool

Bedroom 2
12'-4" X 12'-0"

Master Bath

make-up

Bath 1

Dn.

Linen

Loft

Cove Lighting

WIC

Linen

Bedroom 1
13'-0" X 10'-10"

Open to Below

Deck

His WIC

Her WIC

Master Bedroom
14'-0" X 17'-6"
Tray Ceiling

© THE SATER DESIGN COLLECTION, INC.

2ND FLOOR

The inviting, classic charm of a wraparound porch is where the beauty of Kenton Farms begins. Arches, columns and ceiling treatments define the living space with style and comfort throughout the plan. A substantial leisure room boasts three sets of French doors opening to the back porch and the master suite features its own private deck. Built-ins, spacious walk-ins and a large, accessible kitchen add to the appeal.

3 Bedroom / **3-1/2** Bath

1st Floor: **1,642** sq ft

2nd Floor: **1,205** sq ft

Living Area: **2,847** sq ft

Bonus Room: **340** sq ft

Width: **53'2"**

Depth: **72'0"**

Exterior Walls: **2x6**

Foundation: crawl space

Price Code: **C3**

© THE SATER DESIGN COLLECTION, INC.

REAR ELEVATION

JASPER | 7019

Enjoy the simple, quiet beauty of Jasper — from the column-lined wraparound porch to the decorative shutters and transom windows. Inside, the uniquely designed open kitchen, nook and leisure room create a massive living space with built-ins, fireplace and a coffered ceiling. The master suite features a private deck, walk-in closets and a sitting area. Two secondary bedrooms share a bath and built-in computer desk.

3 Bedroom / **2-1/2** Bath

1st Floor: **1,664** sq ft

2nd Floor: **1,463** sq ft

Living Area: **3,127** sq ft

Width: **59'10"**

Depth: **62'0"**

Exterior Walls: **2x6**

Foundation: crawl space/ opt. basement

Price Code: **C4**

1ST FLOOR

Porch
21'-4" x 15'-4"

Leisure Room
17'-8" x 15'-8"
Coffered Ceiling

Nook
9'-6" x 10'-8"

Built-in

Fireplace

Built-in

Garage
22'-4" x 23'-0"

Kitchen
Island
14'-0" x 12'-8"

Utility

Storage

Dining
12'-10" x 10'-8"
Beamed

Storage

Dn

© THE SATER DESIGN COLLECTION, INC.

Pwdr.

Living
12'-10" x 16'-6"
Stepped

Up

Foyer

Study
11'-0" x 13'-0"

Porch
28'-10" x 8'-0"

2ND FLOOR

Deck

Master Suite
17'-8" x 15'-0"

Sitting

Am Kitchen

Whirlpool

Master Bath

L

Her WIC

WIC

His WIC

Bedroom 2
16'-6 x 12'-0"

Computer Desk

L

Dn

Bath

L

Open to Below

CL

Bedroom 1
11'-0 x 13'-6"

© THE SATER DESIGN COLLECTION, INC.

© THE SATER DESIGN COLLECTION, INC.

7022 | JEFFERSON

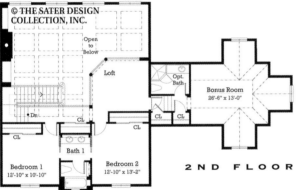

© THE SATER DESIGN COLLECTION, INC.

Open to Below

Loft

Opt. Bath

Bonus Room
26'-6" x 13'-0"

CL

Dn

CL

CL

CL

Bath 1

Bedroom 1
12'-10" x 10'-10"

Bedroom 2
12'-10" x 13'-2"

2ND FLOOR

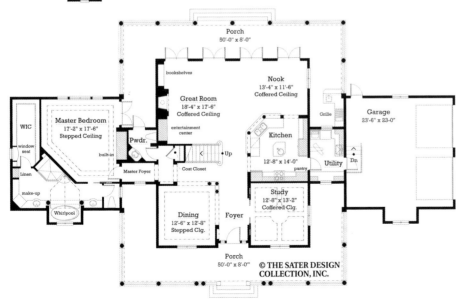

Porch
50'-0" x 8'-0"

bookshelves

Nook
13'-4" x 11'-6"
Coffered Ceiling

Great Room
18'-4" x 17'-6"
Coffered Ceiling

Master Bedroom
17'-2" x 17'-6"
Stepped Ceiling

WIC

entertainment center

Grille

Garage
23'-6" x 23'-0"

window seat

Pwdr.

built-in

Master Foyer

Up

Kitchen
12'-8" x 14'-0"

Utility

Dn

linen

Coat Closet

pantry

make-up

Study
12'-8" x 13'-2"
Coffered Clg.

Whirlpool

Dining
12'-6" x 12'-8"
Stepped Clg.

Foyer

Porch
50'-0" x 8'-0"

© THE SATER DESIGN COLLECTION, INC.

1ST FLOOR

This stunning, sprawling plan features front and rear wraparound porches, tapered columns and multi-paned windows. The spacious interior creates an open, inviting environment through a large loft, open kitchen and great room with French doors that expand your living area outward. Find new options with the unique bonus room and the private foyer and spacious bath in the master retreat.

3 Bedroom / **3-1/2** Bath

1st Floor: **2,151** sq ft

2nd Floor: **722** sq ft

Living Area: **2,873** sq ft

Bonus Room: **498** sq ft

Width: **98'0"**

Depth: **76'0"**

Exterior Walls: **2x6**

Foundation: crawl space/opt. basement

Price Code: **C3**

© THE SATER DESIGN COLLECTION, INC.

REAR ELEVATION

BRICEWOOD | 7025

Square columns and fretwork define Bricewood's classic dormer-topped entry. The open, engaging living space features columns lining the foyer, a sizeable kitchen with walk-in pantry, and a great room boasting a fireplace and art niche. The secluded master retreat is complete with a luxe bath and access to the back porch. Upstairs, secondary bedrooms enjoy a built-in desk and cabinetry.

3 Bedroom / **2-1/2** Bath

1st Floor: **2,073** sq ft

2nd Floor: **869** sq ft

Living Area: **2,942** sq ft

Width: **64'0"**

Depth: **76'2"**

Exterior Walls: **2x6**

Foundation: crawl space/ opt. basement

Price Code: **C3**

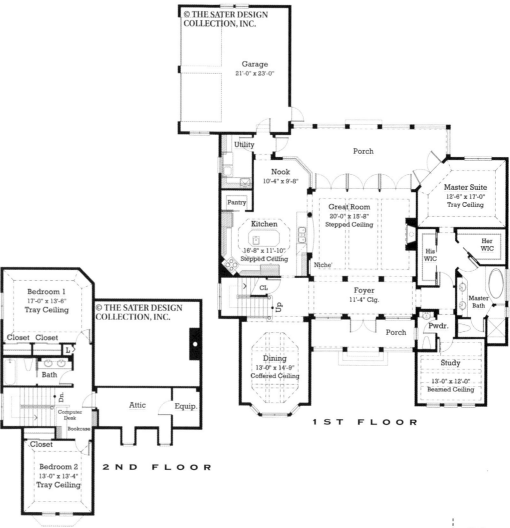

© THE SATER DESIGN COLLECTION, INC.

Garage
21'-0" x 23'-0"

Utility

Porch

Nook
10'-4" x 9'-8"

Master Suite
12'-6" x 17'-0"
Tray Ceiling

Pantry

Great Room
20'-0" x 15'-8"
Stepped Ceiling

Kitchen
16'-8" x 11'-10"
Stepped Ceiling

His WIC

Her WIC

Niche'

Master Bath

CL

Foyer
11'-4" Clg.

Up

Porch

Pwdr.

Dining
13'-0" x 14'-9"
Coffered Ceiling

Study
13'-0" x 12'-0"
Beamed Ceiling

1ST FLOOR

Bedroom 1
17'-0" x 13'-6"
Tray Ceiling

© THE SATER DESIGN COLLECTION, INC.

Closet Closet

Bath

Computer Desk

Attic

Equip.

Bookcase

Closet

Bedroom 2
13'-0" x 13'-4"
Tray Ceiling

2ND FLOOR

© THE SATER DESIGN COLLECTION, INC.

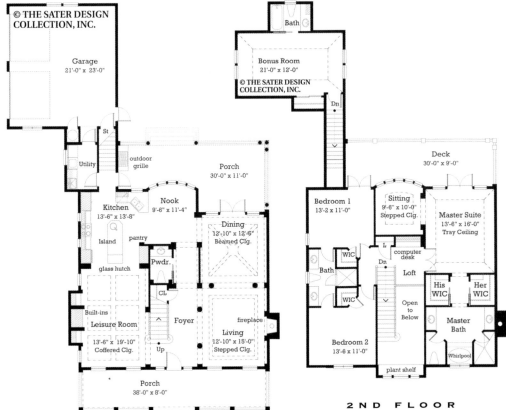

1ST FLOOR

Garage
21'-0" x 23'-0"

St

Utility

outdoor grille

Porch
30'-0" x 11'-0"

Nook
9'-6" x 11'-4"

Kitchen
13'-6" x 13'-8"

Island

pantry

glass hutch

Pwdr.

CL

Dining
12'-10" x 12'-6"
Beamed Clg.

Built-ins

Leisure Room
13'-6" x 19'-10"
Coffered Clg.

Foyer

Up

fireplace

Living
12'-10" x 15'-0"
Stepped Clg.

Porch
38'-0" x 8'-0"

2ND FLOOR

Bath

Bonus Room
21'-0" x 12'-0"

© THE SATER DESIGN
COLLECTION, INC.

Dn

Deck
30'-0" x 9'-0"

Bedroom 1
13'-2 x 11'-0"

Sitting
9'-6" x 10'-0"
Stepped Clg.

Master Suite
13'-6" x 16'-0"
Tray Ceiling

WIC

L

computer desk

Bath

Dn

Loft

WIC

Open to Below

His WIC

Her WIC

Master Bath

Bedroom 2
13'-6 x 11'-0"

Whirlpool

plant shelf

Whether you notice the full-width front porch and multi-paned windows or the big central dormer first, the Kendall invites you in. The open, formal living and dining rooms feature stepped and beamed ceilings and the large kitchen with work island opens wide into the nook and leisure room. Two big bedrooms, an impressive sitting room, a magnificent master suite and even a bonus room are discovered upstairs.

3 Bedroom / **2-1/2** Bath

1st Floor: **1,387** sq ft

2nd Floor: **1,175** sq ft

Living Area: **2,562** sq ft

Bonus Room: **362** sq ft

Width: **54'0"**

Depth: **78'0"**

Exterior Walls: **2x6**

Foundation: crawl space

Price Code: **C3**

© THE SATER DESIGN COLLECTION, INC.

REAR ELEVATION

HOLBROOK | 7031

With twin dormers, mirroring chimneys and a prominent center gable, Holbrook achieves a sense of classic, exquisite symmetry. The eye-catching octagonal great room opens through French doors to the backyard. It is flanked by a formal dining room and open kitchen on one side and an extraordinary master suite with private porch on the other. Secondary bedrooms, a den, loft and more are found upstairs.

3 Bedroom / **3-1/2** Bath

1st Floor: **1,627** sq ft

2nd Floor: **1,024** sq ft

Living Area: **2,651** sq ft

Width: **78'0"**

Depth: **80'6"**

Exterior Walls: **2x6**

Foundation: crawl space/ opt. basement

Price Code: **C3**

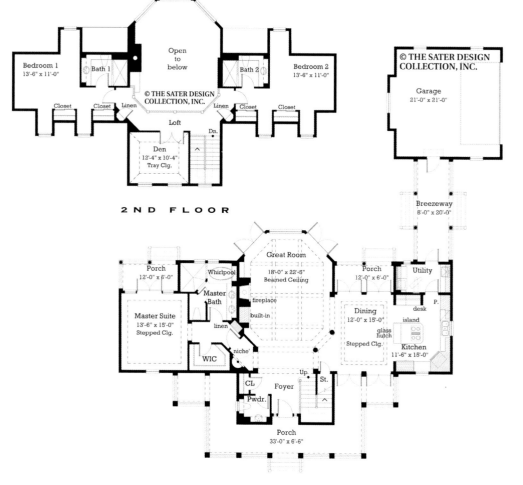

2ND FLOOR

1ST FLOOR

© THE SATER DESIGN COLLECTION, INC.

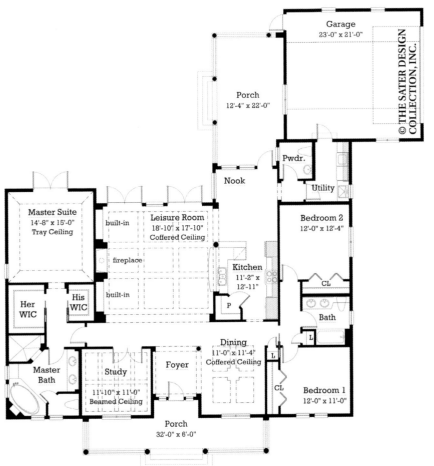

© THE SATER DESIGN COLLECTION, INC.

Garage
23'-0" x 21'-0"

Porch
12'-4" x 22'-0"

Nook

Pwdr.

Utility

Bedroom 2
12'-0" x 12'-4"

Master Suite
14'-8" x 15'-0"
Tray Ceiling

built-in

Leisure Room
18'-10" x 17'-10"
Coffered Ceiling

fireplace

built-in

Kitchen
11'-2" x 12'-11"

CL

Bath

Her WIC

His WIC

P

L

L

Master Bath

Study
11'-10" x 11'-0"
Beamed Ceiling

Foyer

Dining
11'-0" x 11'-4"
Coffered Ceiling

CL

Bedroom 1
12'-0" x 11'-0"

Porch
32'-0" x 6'-0"

REAR ELEVATION

7034 | SOMERVILLE

Find simple sophistication in the pyramid-shaped hip roof, decorative arches and tapered columns of the Somerville façade. Inside, the considerable great room, formal dining room, kitchen and nook all make for an open, flowing quality. A built-in fireplace and cabinetry, multiple sets of French doors, a handsome study and private master suite are all prominently featured.

3 Bedroom / **2-1/2** Bath

Living Area: **2,329** sq ft

Width: **72'6"**

Depth: **73'4"**

Exterior Walls: **2x6**

Foundation: crawl space

Price Code: **C2**

© THE SATER DESIGN COLLECTION, INC.

REAR ELEVATION

LANGFORD | 7037

Asymmetrical rooflines, triple dormers and first- and second-story porches make for Langford's welcoming façade. There's a lot to love in this unique design: the open kitchen with convenient pass-thru; the large leisure room with French doors to the back porch; the formal living and dining rooms set off by stately columns; the private upper floor featuring the master suite and three secondary bedrooms; and more.

4 Bedroom / **2-1/2** Bath

1st Floor: **1,865** sq ft

2nd Floor: **1,477** sq ft

Living Area: **3,342** sq ft

Bonus Room: **282** sq ft

Width: **78'0"**

Depth: **78'8"**

Exterior Walls: **2x6**

Foundation: crawl space/opt. basement

Price Code: **C4**

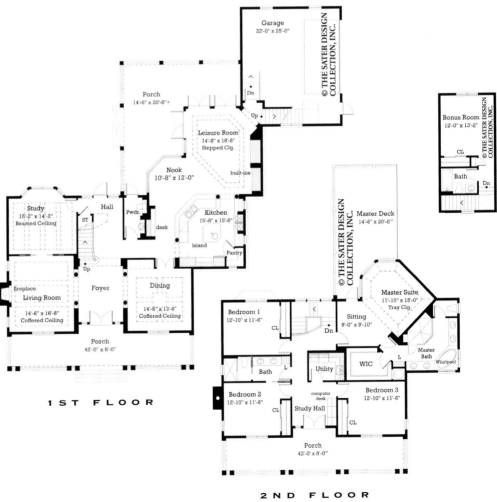

1ST FLOOR

2ND FLOOR

© THE SATER DESIGN COLLECTION, INC.

1ST FLOOR

Porch

Dn

Garage
21'-0" x 23'-0"

Porch

WIC

book shelves
built-ins

Great Room
15'-0" x 20'-6"
Coffered Ceiling

fireplace

Master Suite
11'-6" x 13'-2"
Stepped Clg.

built-ins

book shelves

Outdoor
Grille

© THE SATER DESIGN
COLLECTION, INC.

Kitchen

Nook
9'-6" x 9'-6"
Tray Clg.

island

11'-6" x 13'-2"
Stepped Clg.

Pantry

Utility

M.
Bath

Up

Stor.

Foyer

Dining
15'-0" x 11'-6"
Stepped Ceiling

Pwdr.

Dn

Porch

2ND FLOOR

Deck

Deck

© THE SATER DESIGN
COLLECTION, INC.

Bedroom 1
11'-6" x 13'-2"

Open
to
Below

Bedroom 2
11'-6" x 13'-2"

WIC

Dn

Loft

Computer
Desk

WIC

Bath

REAR ELEVATION

7040 | BAKERSFIELD

Once you've taken in the impressive triple dormers, you'll notice the wraparound front porch is crafted in decorative fretwork. This terrific, open floor plan features exciting details around every corner including stepped and coffered ceilings, built-in shelves and computer desk, a butler's pantry and an outdoor grill. A pair of secondary bedrooms on the upper floor also feature private decks and walk-in closets.

3 Bedroom / **2-1/2** Bath

1st Floor: **1,493** sq ft

2nd Floor: **676** sq ft

Living Area: **2,169** sq ft

Width: **69'6"**

Depth: **55'2"**

Exterior Walls: **2x6**

Foundation: crawl space/
opt. basement

Price Code: **C2**

© THE SATER DESIGN COLLECTION, INC.

REAR ELEVATION

DEERWOOD | 7043

From its high-pitched rooflines down to each classic column lining its porch, Deerwood radiates a comforting sense of home. This floor plan opens out to a massive back porch in four different sets of glass doors, and the kitchen affords easy access to the dining, nook and great rooms. His-and-hers walk-in closets and a spacious master bath enhance the private master suite.

3 Bedroom / **2** Bath

Living Area: **1,989** sq ft

Bonus Room: **291** sq ft

Width: **80'6"**

Depth: **50'0"**

Exterior Walls: **2x6**

Foundation: crawl space/ opt. basement

Price Code: **C1**

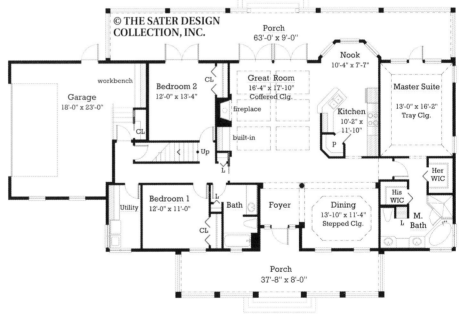

© THE SATER DESIGN COLLECTION, INC.

Porch 63'-0" x 9'-0"

workbench

Garage 18'-0" x 23'-0"

Bedroom 2 12'-0" x 13'-4"

CL

CL

Great Room 16'-4" x 17'-10" Coffered Clg.

fireplace

built-in

Up

L

Nook 10'-4" x 7'-7"

Kitchen 10'-2" x 11'-10"

P

Master Suite 13'-0" x 16'-2" Tray Clg.

Her WIC

His WIC

M. Bath

L

Utility

Bedroom 1 12'-0" x 11'-0"

L

CL

Bath

Foyer

Dining 13'-10" x 11'-4" Stepped Clg.

Porch 37'-8" x 8'-0"

1ST FLOOR

Bonus Room 16'-6" x 11'-0"

Bath

Dn

© THE SATER DESIGN COLLECTION, INC.

2ND FLOOR

© THE SATER DESIGN COLLECTION, INC.

REAR ELEVATION

7046 | ALDEN PINES

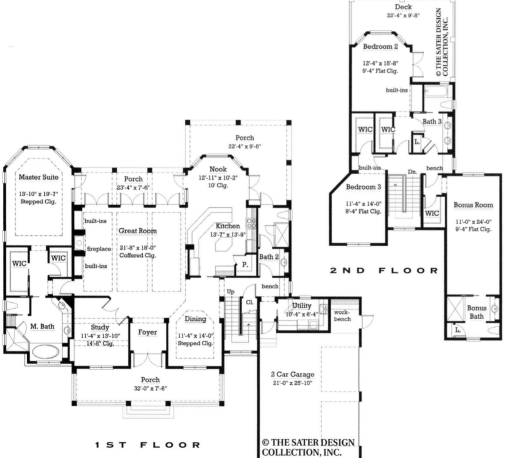

Deck
22'-4" x 9'-8"

Bedroom 2
12'-4" x 15'-8"
9'-4" Flat Clg.

built-ins

WIC | WIC

Bath 3
L.

built-ins

Dn.

bench

Bedroom 3
11'-4" x 14'-0"
9'-4" Flat Clg.

WIC

Bonus Room
11'-0" x 24'-0"
9'-4" Flat Clg.

Bonus Bath
L.

2ND FLOOR

Master Suite
13'-10" x 19'-7"
Stepped Clg.

Porch
23'-4" x 7'-6"

Porch
22'-4" x 9'-8"

Nook
12'-11" x 10'-2"
10' Clg.

built-ins

Great Room
21'-8" x 18'-0"
Coffered Clg.

fireplace

built-ins

Kitchen
13'-7" x 13'-9"

P.

Bath 2

WIC | WIC

M. Bath

Study
11'-4" x 13'-10"
14'-8" Clg.

Foyer

Dining
11'-4" x 14'-0"
Stepped Clg.

Up

Cl.

bench

Utility
10'-4" x 6'-4"

work-bench

Porch
32'-0" x 7'-6"

2 Car Garage
21'-0" x 25'-10"

1ST FLOOR

© THE SATER DESIGN
COLLECTION, INC.

Simple columns and hipped gables display the character of a classic country estate. Past the foyer, the spacious great room accesses the back porch through three sets of French doors. The kitchen boasts a wraparound eating bar and easy, open entry to the nook and formal dining room. A large study with built-ins, private master suite and ample living area on the upper level add to the design's appeal.

3 Bedroom / **3** Bath

1st Floor: **2,215** sq ft

2nd Floor: **708** sq ft

Living Area: **2,923** sq ft

Bonus Room: **461** sq ft

Width: **75'4"**

Depth: **69'4"**

Exterior Walls: **2x6**

Foundation: crawl space/
opt. basement

Price Code: **C3**

© THE SATER DESIGN COLLECTION, INC.

REAR ELEVATION

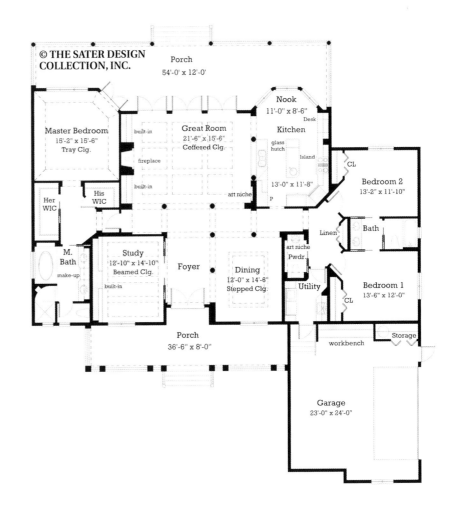

MONTGOMERY | 7049

A prominent hipped gable elevates from a classic column-lined entry porch. Montgomery is an especially open floor plan with large dining, kitchen and great rooms divided by columns. Three sets of French doors open the great room to the back porch; another set is found in the master bedroom. This split floor plan affords easy privacy for the master suite.

3 Bedroom / **2-1/2** Bath

Living Area: **2,555** sq ft

Width: **70'0"**

Depth: **76'6"**

Exterior Walls: **2x6**

Foundation: crawl space

Price Code: **C3**

© THE SATER DESIGN COLLECTION, INC.

Porch
54'-0" x 12'-0"

Master Bedroom
15'-2" x 15'-6"
Tray Clg.

built-in

fireplace

built-in

Great Room
21'-6" x 15'-6"
Coffered Clg.

Nook
11'-0" x 8'-6"

Desk

Kitchen

glass
hutch

Island

13'-0" x 11'-8"

CL

art niche

P

Bedroom 2
13'-2" x 11'-10"

Her
WIC

His
WIC

M.
Bath

make-up

Study
12'-10" x 14'-10"
Beamed Clg.

built-in

Foyer

Dining
12'-0" x 14'-6"
Stepped Clg.

art niche

Pwdr.

Linen

Bath

Utility

CL

Bedroom 1
13'-6" x 12'-0"

Porch
36'-6" x 8'-0"

workbench

Storage

Garage
23'-0" x 24'-0"

© THE SATER DESIGN COLLECTION, INC.

7052 | SHELBY

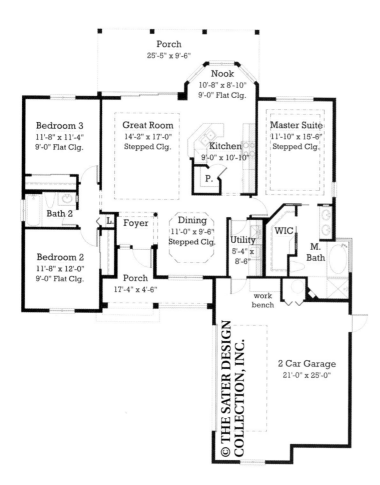

Porch
25'-5" x 9'-6"

Nook
10'-8" x 8'-10"
9'-0" Flat Clg.

Bedroom 3
11'-8" x 11'-4"
9'-0" Flat Clg.

Great Room
14'-2" x 17'-0"
Stepped Clg.

Kitchen
9'-0" x 10'-10"

Master Suite
11'-10" x 15'-6"
Stepped Clg.

P.

Bath 2

L.

Foyer

Dining
11'-0" x 9'-6"
Stepped Clg.

Utility
5'-4" x
8'-6"

WIC

M. Bath

Bedroom 2
11'-8" x 12'-0"
9'-0" Flat Clg.

Porch
17'-4" x 4'-6"

work bench

© THE SATER DESIGN COLLECTION, INC.

2 Car Garage
21'-0" x 25'-0"

Charming gables, twin dormers and lots of curb appeal are found in the simple, classic design of Shelby. The open floor plan, combined with stepped ceilings, presents the overall living area as generous and inviting. The kitchen includes a convenient eating bar and open access to the nook, dining and great rooms. The private master suite with walk-in closet and large bath are separated from two other secondary bedrooms.

3 Bedroom / **2** Bath

Living Area: **1,487** sq ft

Width: **52'0"**

Depth: **65'6"**

Exterior Walls: **2x6**

Foundation: crawl space

Price Code: **A4**

REAR ELEVATION

© THE SATER DESIGN COLLECTION, INC.

WHEATFIELD | 7055

The circular porch, with two-story turret and abundant rectangular windows, makes for a stunning first impression of the Wheatfield. Inside, the grand radius staircase and open ceiling to the second floor reveal ample light, views and impressive details. A formal dining room connects via butler's pantry to the gourmet kitchen, and the large, open floor plan features a big leisure room and private master suite with separate foyer.

4 Bedroom / **3-1/2** Bath

1st Floor: **2,083** sq ft

2nd Floor: **1,013** sq ft

Living Area: **3,096** sq ft

Width: **74'0"**

Depth: **88'0"**

Exterior Walls: **2x6**

Foundation: crawl space

Price Code: **C4**

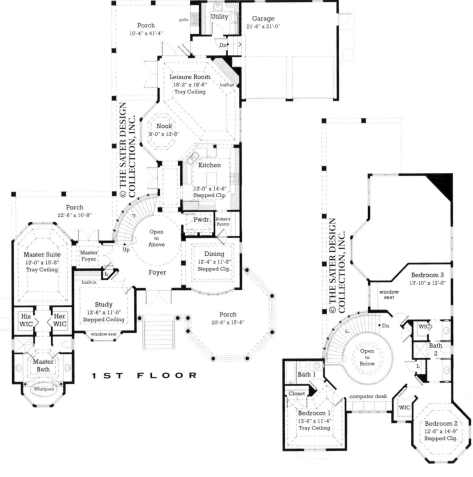

1ST FLOOR

2ND FLOOR

© THE SATER DESIGN COLLECTION, INC.

7058 | CLOVERDALE

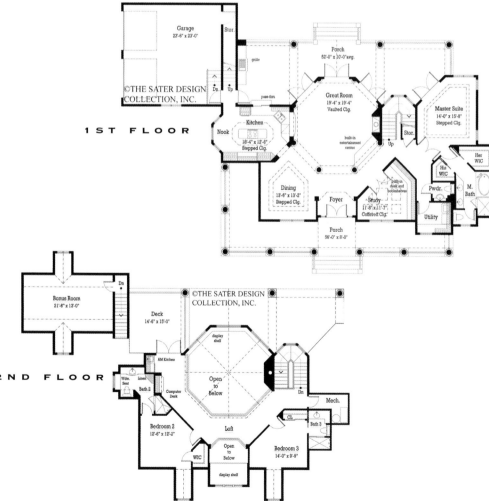

1ST FLOOR

©THE SATER DESIGN
COLLECTION, INC.

Garage
23'-6" x 23'-0"

Stor.

grille

pass-thru

Dn. Up

Porch
52'-0" x 10'-0" avg.

Great Room
19'-4" x 19'-4"
Vaulted Clg.

built-in
entertainment
center

Up Stor.

Master Suite
14'-0" x 15'-8"
Stepped Clg.

Kitchen
18'-4" x 12'-6"
Stepped Clg.

Nook

Her
WIC

His
WIC

Dining
13'-6" x 13'-2"
Stepped Clg.

Foyer

Study
11'-6" x 11'-7"
Coffered Clg.

built-in
desk and
bookshelves

Pwdr.

Utility

M.
Bath

Porch
56'-0" x 8'-0"

2ND FLOOR

Bonus Room
21'-6" x 13'-0"

Dn.

Deck
14'-6" x 15'-0"

©THE SATER DESIGN
COLLECTION, INC.

display
shelf

AM Kitchen

Wdw.
Seat

linen

Bath 2

Computer
Desk

Open
to
Below

Dn.

Mech.

Cl.

Bath 3

Bedroom 2
12'-6" x 13'-0"

Loft

Open
to
Below

Bedroom 3
14'-0" x 9'-9"

WIC

display shelf

The big, wraparound porch and dormer windows add a sense of graceful appeal to Cloverdale. A generous, octagonal-shaped great room with fireplace and three sets of French doors to the back porch centers this large, open floor plan. A formal dining room and gourmet kitchen with pass-thru to the back porch make entertaining easy. A handsome study, private master suite, two guest bedrooms and a bonus room add to the appeal.

3 Bedroom / **3-1/2** Bath

1st Floor: **1,874** sq ft

2nd Floor: **901** sq ft

Living Area: **2,775** sq ft

Bonus Room: **382** sq ft

Width: **90'0"**

Depth: **58'6"**

Exterior Walls: **2x6**

Foundation: crawl space/opt basement

Price Code: **C3**

© THE SATER DESIGN COLLECTION, INC.

REAR ELEVATION

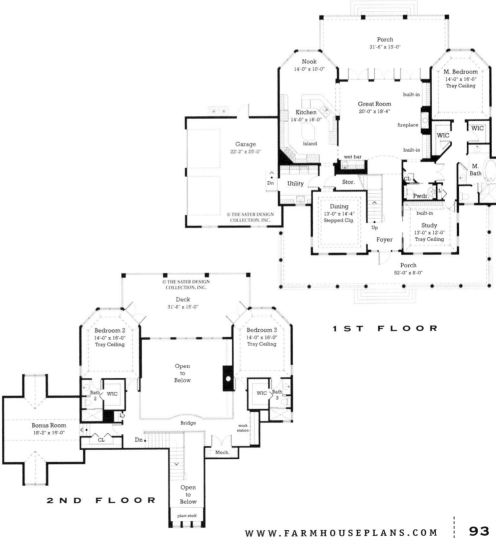

KENNEDY | 7061

Expand your living space outward with Kennedy's engaging wraparound porch and multi-level rear decks. A big, welcoming great room — with multiple sets of French doors — features built-ins and open access to the kitchen and nook. Double doors access the master retreat, which also reveals a private study. Upstairs, two guest bedrooms, each with large baths and walk-in closets, adjoin a spacious bonus room.

3 Bedroom / **3-1/2** Bath

1st Floor: **2,138** sq ft

2nd Floor: **944** sq ft

Living Area: **3,082** sq ft

Bonus Room: **427** sq ft

Width: **76'8"**

Depth: **64'0"**

Exterior Walls: **2x6**

Foundation: crawl space/opt. basement

Price Code: **C4**

1ST FLOOR

Porch 31'-6" x 15'-0"
Nook 14'-0" x 10'-0"
M. Bedroom 14'-0" x 16'-0" Tray Ceiling
Great Room 20'-0" x 18'-4"
Kitchen 14'-0" x 16'-0"
Garage 22'-2" x 25'-0"
Island
wet bar
WIC
WIC
M. Bath
built-in
fireplace
built-in
Utility
Stor.
CL
Pwdr.
Dn
Dining 13'-0" x 14'-4" Stepped Clg.
built-in
Study 13'-0" x 12'-0" Tray Ceiling
Up
Foyer
Porch 52'-0" x 8'-0"
© THE SATER DESIGN COLLECTION, INC.

2ND FLOOR

© THE SATER DESIGN COLLECTION, INC.
Deck 31'-6" x 15'-0"
Bedroom 2 14'-0" x 16'-0" Tray Ceiling
Bedroom 3 14'-0" x 16'-0" Tray Ceiling
Open to Below
Bath 2
WIC
WIC
Bath 3
Bonus Room 18'-2" x 16'-0"
CL
Dn
Bridge
work station
Mech.
Open to Below
plant shelf

© THE SATER DESIGN COLLECTION, INC.

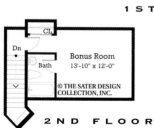

REAR ELEVATION

7064 | MADISON

1ST FLOOR

Garage
19'-2" x 23'-0"

Stor.

Up

Dn

Utility

Dining
11'-4" x 14'-0"
Stepped Clg.

desk

Master Suite
13'-0" x 19'-6"
Tray Clg.

Porch
32'-4" x 8'-0"

bookshelves

ent. center

Study
12'-4" x 13'-0"
Stepped Clg.

built-in

Great Room
18'-4" x 19'-0"
Coffered Clg.

double-sided
fireplace

built-in

bookshelves

Kitchen
14'-4" x 13'-8"

island

Stepped Clg.

P

Bedroom 2
11'-2" x 11'-6"

CL

Bath

CL

L

Her
WIC

His
WIC

L   make-up

Master Bath

Whirlpool

Foyer

Porch
20'-8" x 8'-0"

Bedroom 1
12'-8" x 11'-8"

CL

CL

2ND FLOOR

CL

Dn

Bath

Bonus Room
13'-10" x 12'-0"

© THE SATER DESIGN
COLLECTION, INC.

This stately plan exhibits clean, classic lines in the front-porch pillars and dual-vented dormers. The substantial great room features a coffered ceiling, built-ins and open access to the kitchen and dining rooms. The great room and study share a double-sided fireplace, and both rooms boast French-door access to the rear porch — as does the sizeable master suite. Madison also features a luxurious master bath, bonus room and more.

3 Bedroom / **2** Bath

Living Area: **2,454** sq ft

Bonus Room: **256** sq ft

Width: **80'6"**

Depth: **66'0"**

Exterior Walls: **2x6**

Foundation: crawl space

Price Code: **C2**

REAR ELEVATION

SOUTHINGTON | 7067

Enduring charm radiates from the multi-paned dormer windows and welcoming front porch of Southington. Inside, stepped and tray ceilings define this open, bright floor plan that features a private master suite with luxury bath; generous dining and great rooms with multiple sets of French doors to the back porch; kitchen with useful eating bar; and, above the garage, a bonus room offering many possible options.

3 Bedroom / **2** Bath

Living Area: **1,616** sq ft

Bonus Room: **362** sq ft

Width: **64'0"**

Depth: **54'6"**

Exterior Walls: **2x6**

Foundation: crawl space

Price Code: **C1**

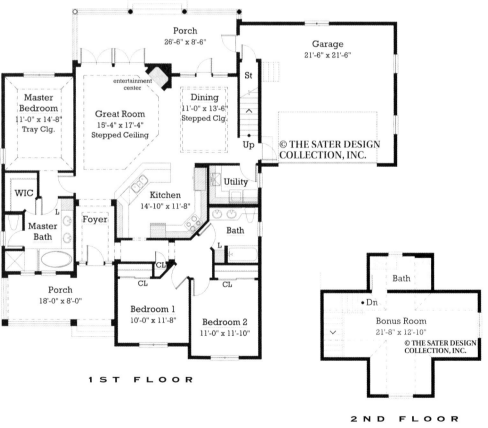

1ST FLOOR

2ND FLOOR

© THE SATER DESIGN COLLECTION, INC.

7073 | WESTBURY

Consider Westbury's handsome façade, flanked by a box-bay window and a single, bright dormer. The foyer unfolds into the dining and great rooms, with instant views through to the back porch. The master suite also opens to the back porch through French doors. A gourmet kitchen features a pass-thru to the great room, and a bonus room over the garage offers even more opportunities to expand your living space.

3 Bedroom / **2** Bath

Living Area: **1,526** sq ft

Bonus Room: **336** sq ft

Width: **64'0"**

Depth: **54'0"**

Exterior Walls: **2x6**

Foundation: crawl space

Price Code: **C1**

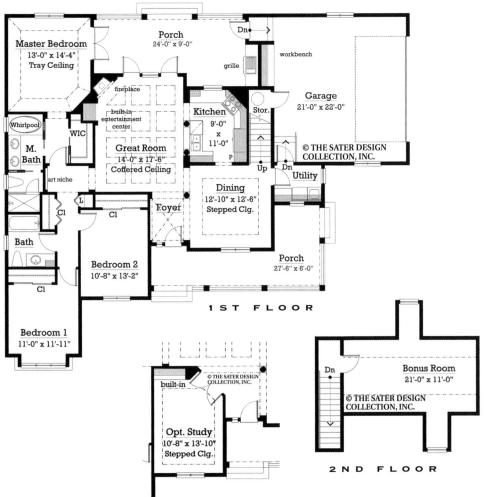

Master Bedroom 13'-0" x 14'-4" Tray Ceiling

Porch 24'-0" x 9'-0"

Dn

workbench

grille

fireplace

built-in entertainment center

Whirlpool

WIC

Kitchen 9'-0" x 11'-0"

Stor.

Garage 21'-0" x 22'-0"

© THE SATER DESIGN COLLECTION, INC.

M. Bath

Great Room 14'-0" x 17'-6" Coffered Ceiling

art niche

Up

Dn

Utility

Cl

L

Cl

Foyer

Dining 12'-10" x 12'-6" Stepped Clg.

Bath

Bedroom 2 10'-8" x 13'-2"

Cl

Porch 27'-6" x 6'-0"

Bedroom 1 11'-0" x 11'-11"

1ST FLOOR

built-in

© THE SATER DESIGN COLLECTION, INC.

Opt. Study 10'-8" x 13'-10" Stepped Clg.

Dn

Bonus Room 21'-0" x 11'-0"

© THE SATER DESIGN COLLECTION, INC.

2ND FLOOR

© THE SATER DESIGN COLLECTION, INC.

REAR ELEVATION

LAUREL LAKE | 7075

The detailed fretwork and gable, along with fish-scale siding, enhance the façade of Laurel Lake. The foyer unfolds into the dining and great rooms, with instant views through to the back porch. The master suite also opens to the back porch through glass doors. A gourmet kitchen features a pass-thru to the great room, and a bonus room over the garage offers even more opportunities to expand your living space.

3 Bedroom / **2** Bath

Living Area: **1,526** sq ft

Bonus Room: **336** sq ft

Width: **65'0"**

Depth: **54'6"**

Exterior Walls: **2x6**

Foundation: crawl space

Price Code: **C1**

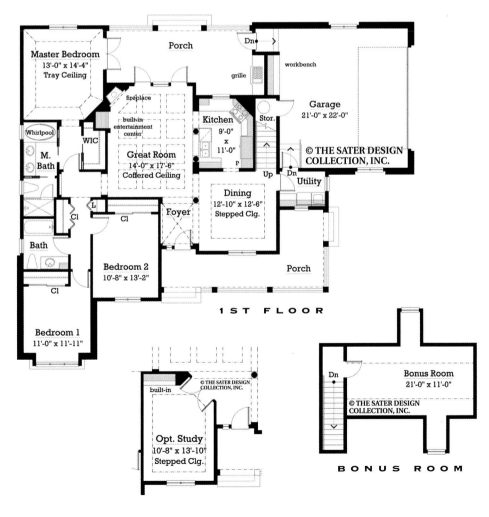

1ST FLOOR

Master Bedroom 13'-0" x 14'-4" Tray Ceiling

Porch

workbench

grille

Garage 21'-0" x 22'-0"

Whirlpool

M. Bath

WIC

fireplace

built-in entertainment center

Great Room 14'-0" x 17'-6" Coffered Ceiling

Kitchen 9'-0" x 11'-0"

Stor.

© THE SATER DESIGN COLLECTION, INC.

Up

Dn

Utility

Bath

Cl

L

Cl

Foyer

Dining 12'-10" x 12'-6" Stepped Clg.

Bedroom 2 10'-8" x 13'-2"

Porch

Cl

Bedroom 1 11'-0" x 11'-11"

built-in

© THE SATER DESIGN COLLECTION, INC.

Opt. Study 10'-8" x 13'-10" Stepped Clg.

Dn

Bonus Room 21'-0" x 11'-0"

© THE SATER DESIGN COLLECTION, INC.

BONUS ROOM

© THE SATER DESIGN COLLECTION, INC.

Home photographed may differ then construction documents.

REAR VIEW

7077 | MAPLETON

A sweeping front porch invites all to enjoy gracious Southern living in this creative home filled with Old-World craftsmanship, expansive windows, varied ceiling treatments and a grand verandah with an outdoor fireplace. Guests are pampered with bedroom suites, a custom-designed study for quiet reading and productive work time, and an airy great room and kitchen for festive gatherings of family and friends.

3 Bedroom / **3-1/2** Bath

Living Area: **2,888** sq ft

Width: **72'0"**

Depth: **80'0"**

Exterior Walls: **2x6**

Foundation: crawl space

Price Code: **C3**

© THE SATER DESIGN COLLECTION, INC.

REAR ELEVATION

CHANNING | 8005

This cozy Classic Country-style home employs gentle slump-arches and a copper-topped porch to create an appealing front façade. Split bedrooms bookend formal and casual living areas that are defined by columns and ceiling details. A rear porch opens the views and extends the living areas along the back of the home.

4 Bedroom / **3-1/2** Bath

1st Floor: **2,222** sq ft

2nd Floor: **1,075** sq ft

Living Area: **3,297** sq ft

Bonus Room: **405** sq ft

Width: **91'0"**

Depth: **52'8"**

Exterior Walls: **2x6**

Foundation: slab

Price Code: **C4**

French Country

From fashion to wine, film and art, French culture and design have influenced an international aesthetic of style, romance and elegance. A timeless spirit of diversity and innovation thrives in French design, enticing us to approach and enjoy the charm and drama of its Old-World appeal. These striking French Country designs represent a blending of old and new — of natural stone textures, gracefully curved arches, picturesque Tuscan columns and dazzling, beautiful façades. And deep rustic charm can be found in the open, flowing floor plans, impressive ceiling treatments, gorgeous sunburst windows and multiple French doors opening up to sprawling wrap-around porches. Look further inside to find stunning great rooms with stone fireplaces and multiple built-ins; stylish, open kitchens with all the amenities; and substantial baths and private master suites, all suited to your sense of the extraordinaire.

© THE SATER DESIGN COLLECTION, INC.

REAR ELEVATION

HERON CREEK | 7002

Dormers, tapered columns and a split-shake roof characterize Heron Creek with strong, rustic appeal. This roomy, private floor plan features an open kitchen with large pantry and nook, and the spacious family room is flanked by a wet bar and built-in entertainment center. A huge walk-in closet and master bath, along with French doors to the back porch, make for an impressive and private master suite.

3 Bedroom / **2** Bath

Living Area: **1,848** sq ft

Width: **58'0"**

Depth: **60'0"**

Exterior Walls: **2x6**

Foundation: crawl space

Price Code: **C1**

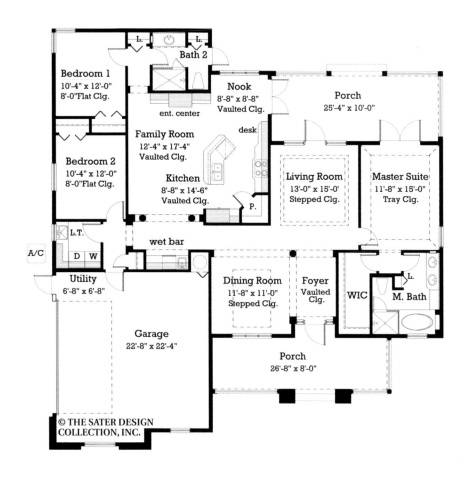

© THE SATER DESIGN COLLECTION, INC.

© THE SATER DESIGN COLLECTION, INC.

7005 | MARCELLA

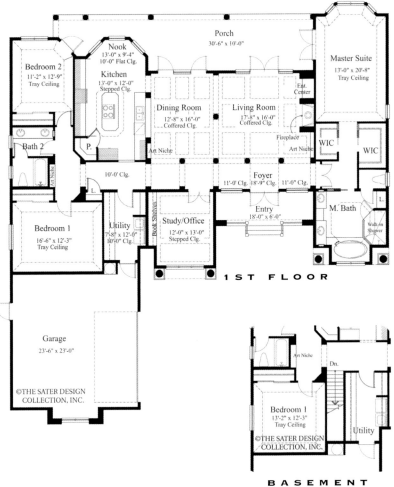

Porch
30'-6" x 10'-0"

Nook
13'-0" x 9'-4"
10'-0" Flat Clg.

Bedroom 2
11'-2" x 12'-9"
Tray Ceiling

Kitchen
13'-0" x 12'-0"
Stepped Clg.

Master Suite
13'-0" x 20'-8"
Tray Ceiling

Ent.
Center

Dining Room
12'-8" x 16'-0"
Coffered Clg.

Living Room
17'-8" x 16'-0"
Coffered Clg.

Fireplace

Bath 2

Art Niche

Art Niche

WIC

WIC

10'-0" Clg.

Foyer
11'-0" Clg.   18'-9" Clg.   11'-0" Clg.

Bedroom 1
16'-6" x 12'-3"
Tray Ceiling

Utility
7'-8" x 12'-0"
10'-0" Clg.

Book Shelves

Study/Office
12'-0" x 13'-0"
Stepped Clg.

Entry
18'-0" x 6'-0"

M. Bath

Walk-in
Shower

1ST FLOOR

Garage
23'-6" x 23'-0"

©THE SATER DESIGN
COLLECTION, INC.

Art Niche

Dn.

Bedroom 1
13'-2" x 12'-3"
Tray Ceiling

Utility

©THE SATER DESIGN
COLLECTION, INC.

**BASEMENT
STAIR OPTION**

An expansive rear porch and recessed arched covered entryway are the highlights of Marcella. Inside, more columns and coffered ceilings provide understated elegance to the living and dining rooms. With its handy pass-thru to the dining room, the kitchen also features a walk-in pantry and spacious nook. Enjoy the view through a wall of windows from the office or exit the generous master suite through French doors.

3 Bedroom / **2** Bath

Living Area: **2,487** sq ft

Width: **70'0"**

Depth: **72'0"**

Exterior Walls: **2x6**

Foundation: slab/
opt. basement

Price Code: **C2**

© THE SATER DESIGN COLLECTION, INC.

REAR ELEVATION

ALLEGRA | 7008

The square columns and distinctive Palladian and bay windows all compete for your immediate attention. The plan's centerpiece — an impressive, open great room — features a fireplace, built-in cabinetry and French doors under a vaulted beamed ceiling. A pair of spare bedrooms features built-in desks and walk-in closets. A stepped ceiling, double walk-in closets and a lavish bath complement the master suite.

3 Bedroom / **3** Bath

1st Floor: **1,710** sq ft

2nd Floor: **618** sq ft

Living Area: **2,328** sq ft

Width: **47'0"**

Depth: **50'0"**

Exterior Walls: **2x6**

Foundation: crawl space/ opt. basement

Price Code: **C2**

© THE SATER DESIGN COLLECTION, INC.

7011 | CHANTEL

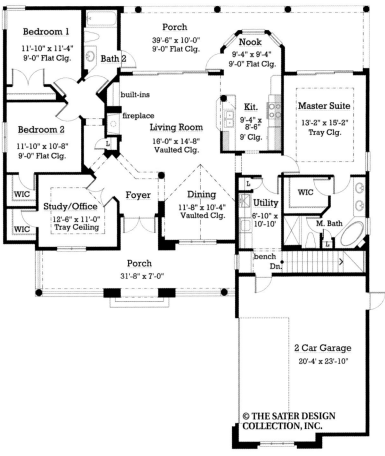

Bedroom 1
11'-10" x 11'-4"
9'-0" Flat Clg.

Bath 2

Porch
39'-6" x 10'-0"
9'-0" Flat Clg.

Nook
9'-4" x 9'-4"
9'-0" Flat Clg.

built-ins

fireplace

Kit.
9'-4" x
8'-6"
9' Clg.

Master Suite
13'-2" x 15'-2"
Tray Clg.

Bedroom 2
11'-10" x 10'-8"
9'-0" Flat Clg.

Living Room
16'-0" x 14'-8"
Vaulted Clg.

WIC

Study/Office
12'-6" x 11'-0"
Tray Ceiling

WIC

Foyer

Dining
11'-8" x 10'-4"
Vaulted Clg.

Utility
6'-10" x
10'-10'

WIC

M. Bath

bench
Dn.

Porch
31'-8" x 7'-0"

2 Car Garage
20'-4' x 23'-10"

© THE SATER DESIGN
COLLECTION, INC.

Enter the covered front porch through a stunning, recessed arched stone gable and you know that Chantel is something special. This open, airy plan features a vaulted ceiling in the living room as well as built-in cabinetry, a fireplace and retreating glass doors. The kitchen nook and master suite both open to the back porch, and the plan's study could easily function as a fourth bedroom.

3 Bedroom / **2** Bath

Living Area: **1,822** sq ft

Width: **58'0"**

Depth: **67'2"**

Exterior Walls: **2x6**

Foundation: basement

Price Code: **C1**

© THE SATER DESIGN COLLECTION, INC.

AVELINE | 7014

The gorgeous façade of Aveline is created through remarkable Palladian and bay windows, decorative shutters, and a dormer. This open floor plan offers elegant columns, impressive built-in cabinetry, kitchen work island and pass-thru, and even a bonus room with separate entry. A secluded master suite, pampering master bath and multiple sets of French doors add to the appeal.

3 Bedroom / **4-1/2** Bath

1st Floor: **1,834** sq ft

2nd Floor: **732** sq ft

Living Area: **2,566** sq ft

Bonus Room: **379** sq ft

Width: **79'0"**

Depth: **50'0"**

Exterior Walls: **2x6**

Foundation: crawl space/ opt. basement

Price Code: **C3**

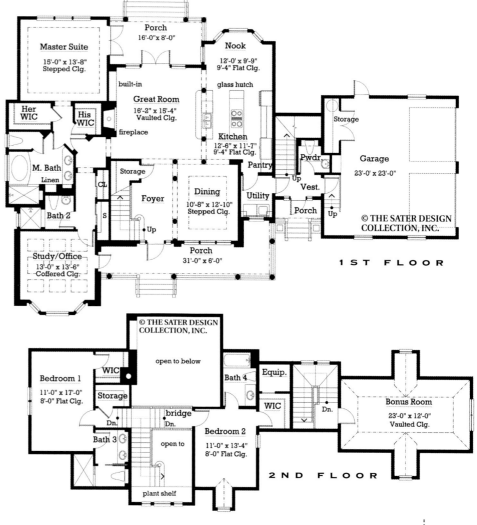

© THE SATER DESIGN COLLECTION, INC.

1ST FLOOR

2ND FLOOR

© THE SATER DESIGN COLLECTION, INC.

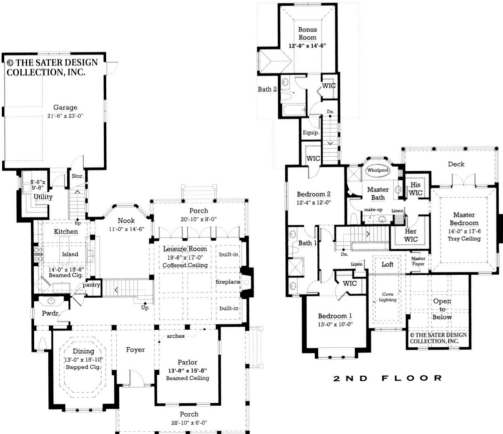

1ST FLOOR

2ND FLOOR

7017 | **SIDONIA**

Sidonia catches the eye with a grand two-story wall of windows and handsome tapered columns. Arches, columns and ceiling treatments define the living space with style and comfort throughout the plan. A substantial leisure room boasts three sets of French doors opening to the back porch and the master suite features its own private deck. Built-ins, spacious walk-ins and a large, accessible kitchen add to the appeal.

3 Bedroom / **3-1/2** Bath

1st Floor: **1,642** sq ft

2nd Floor: **1,205** sq ft

Living Area: **2,847** sq ft

Bonus Room: **340** sq ft

Width: **53'7"**

Depth: **72'6"**

Exterior Walls: **2x6**

Foundation: crawl space

Price Code: **C3**

© THE SATER DESIGN COLLECTION, INC.

REAR ELEVATION

SORRELL GROVE | 7020

The Old-World shutters, casement windows and gables lend a comforting sense of time and place to Sorrell Grove. Inside, the uniquely designed open kitchen, nook and leisure room create a massive living space with built-ins, fireplace and a beamed coffered ceiling. The master suite features a private deck, walk-in closets and sitting area. Two secondary bedrooms share a bath and built-in computer desk.

3 Bedroom / **2-1/2** Bath

1st Floor: **1,673** sq ft

2nd Floor: **1,463** sq ft

Living Area: **3,136** sq ft

Width: **60'10"**

Depth: **62'0"**

Exterior Walls: **2x6**

Foundation: crawl space/ opt. basement

Price Code: **C4**

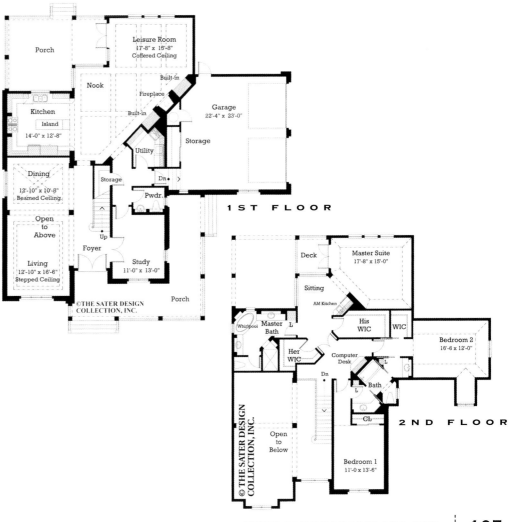

1ST FLOOR

2ND FLOOR

©THE SATER DESIGN COLLECTION, INC.

©THE SATER DESIGN COLLECTION, INC.

© THE SATER DESIGN COLLECTION, INC.

REAR ELEVATION

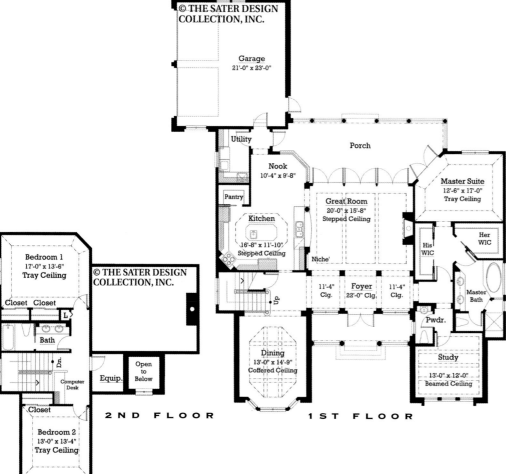

7026 | JULIAN

© THE SATER DESIGN COLLECTION, INC.

Garage
21'-0" x 23'-0"

Utility

Nook
10'-4" x 9'-8"

Porch

Pantry

Kitchen
16'-8" x 11'-10"
Stepped Ceiling

Great Room
20'-0" x 15'-8"
Stepped Ceiling

Master Suite
12'-6" x 17'-0"
Tray Ceiling

His WIC

Her WIC

Niche'

Foyer
22'-0" Clg.

11'-4" Clg.

11'-4" Clg.

Master Bath

Pwdr.

Dining
13'-0" x 14'-9"
Coffered Ceiling

Study
13'-0" x 12'-0"
Beamed Ceiling

Up

1ST FLOOR

Bedroom 1
17'-0" x 13'-6"
Tray Ceiling

© THE SATER DESIGN COLLECTION, INC.

Closet   Closet

Bath

Dn.

Computer Desk

Equip.

Open to Below

Closet

Bedroom 2
13'-0" x 13'-4"
Tray Ceiling

2ND FLOOR

Find casual, but elegant style in Julian with its asymmetrical gables, multi-pane windows and sunburst transoms. The engaging living space features columns lining the foyer, a sizeable kitchen with walk-in pantry, and a great room boasting a fireplace and art niche. The secluded master retreat is complete with a luxurious bath and French-door access to the back porch. Upstairs, two secondary bedrooms enjoy a built-in desk and cabinetry.

3 Bedroom / **2-1/2** Bath

1st Floor: **2,073** sq ft

2nd Floor: **682** sq ft

Living Area: **2,755** sq ft

Width: **64'0"**

Depth: **76'2"**

Exterior Walls: **2x6**

Foundation: crawl space/ opt. basement

Price Code: **C3**

REAR ELEVATION

CHARISSA | 7029

Decorative shutters and handsome stonework lend an inviting, casual warmth to the Charissa plan. The open, formal living and dining rooms feature stepped and beamed ceilings and the large kitchen with work island opens wide into the nook and leisure room. Two big bedrooms, an impressive sitting room, a magnificent master suite and even a bonus room are discovered upstairs.

3 Bedroom / **2-1/2** Bath

1st Floor: **1,387** sq ft

2nd Floor: **1,175** sq ft

Living Area: **2,562** sq ft

Bonus Room: **362** sq ft

Width: **54'0"**

Depth: **78'6"**

Exterior Walls: **2x6**

Foundation: crawl space

Price Code: **C3**

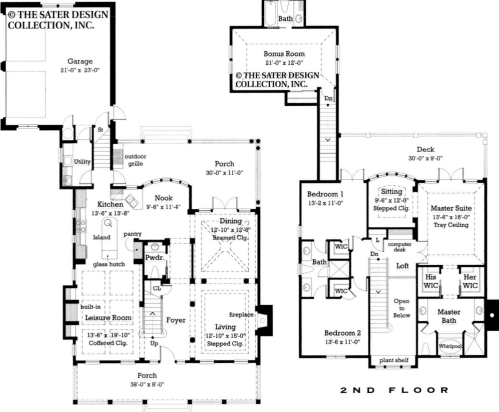

1ST FLOOR

2ND FLOOR

© THE SATER DESIGN COLLECTION, INC.

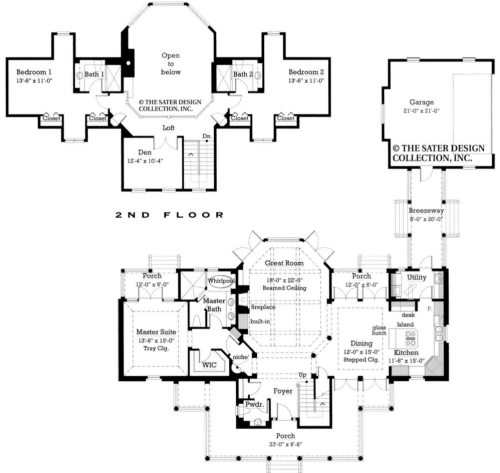

2ND FLOOR

Bedroom 1
13'-6" x 11'-0"

Bath 1

© THE SATER DESIGN
COLLECTION, INC.

Bath 2

Bedroom 2
13'-6" x 11'-0"

Closet Closet Closet Closet

Open to below

Loft

Den
12'-4" x 10'-4"

Dn.

Garage
21'-0" x 21'-0"

© THE SATER DESIGN
COLLECTION, INC.

Breezeway
8'-0" x 20'-0"

1ST FLOOR

Porch
12'-0" x 6'-0"

Whirlpool

Master Bath

Master Suite
13'-6" x 15'-0"
Tray Clg.

WIC

niche

Great Room
18'-0" x 22'-8"
Beamed Ceiling

fireplace

built-in

Porch
12'-0" x 6'-0"

Utility

desk

P.

Island

glass hutch

Dining
12'-0" x 15'-0"
Stepped Clg.

Kitchen
11'-6" x 15'-0"

Up

Foyer

Pwdr.

Porch
33'-0" x 6'-6"

7032 | MERCHAN

From the stone textures, twin dormers and prominent center hip, Merchan achieves a sense of Old-World romance. The octagonal great room opens through French doors to the backyard. It is flanked by a formal dining room and open kitchen on one side and an extraordinary master suite with private porch on the other. Secondary bedrooms, a den, loft and more are found upstairs.

3 Bedroom / **3-1/2** Bath

1st Floor: **1,627** sq ft

2nd Floor: **999** sq ft

Living Area: **2,626** sq ft

Width: **78'6"**

Depth: **80'6"**

Exterior Walls: **2x6**

Foundation: crawl space/ opt. basement

Price Code: **C3**

© THE SATER DESIGN COLLECTION, INC.

REAR ELEVATION

MEDORO | 7035

Find the elegance of French Country-style in the repeating arches, stately columns and high-pitched roof of the Medoro façade. Inside, the considerable leisure room, formal dining room, kitchen and nook all make for an open, flowing quality. A built-in fireplace and cabinetry, multiple sets of French doors, handsome study and master suite are all prominently featured.

3 Bedroom / **2-1/2** Bath

Living Area: **2,329** sq ft

Width: **72'0"**

Depth: **73'4"**

Exterior Walls: **2x6**

Foundation: crawl space

Price Code: **C2**

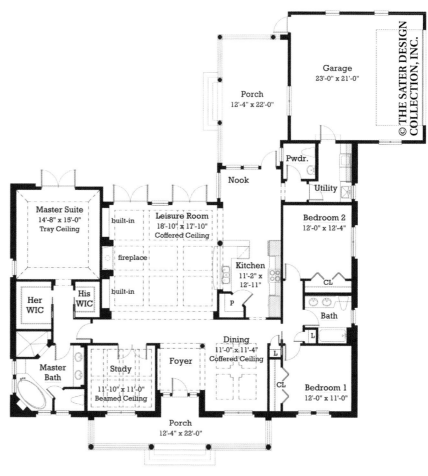

© THE SATER DESIGN COLLECTION, INC.

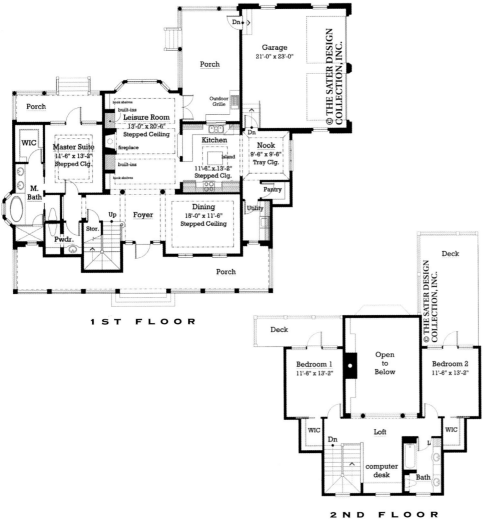

1ST FLOOR

2ND FLOOR

REAR ELEVATION

7041 | DIAMANTA

Diamanta exhibits a striking center hip with a trio of windows and tapered columns lining the wraparound porch. This terrific, open floor plan features exciting details around every corner including stepped and tray ceilings, built-in shelves and computer desk, a butler's pantry and an outdoor grill. A pair of secondary bedrooms on the upper floor also feature private decks and walk-in closets.

3 Bedroom / **2-1/2** Bath

1st Floor: **1,493** sq ft

2nd Floor: **723** sq ft

Living Area: **2,216** sq ft

Width: **70'0"**

Depth: **55'8"**

Exterior Walls: **2x6**

Foundation: crawl space/ opt. basement

Price Code: **C2**

© THE SATER DESIGN COLLECTION, INC.

REAR ELEVATION

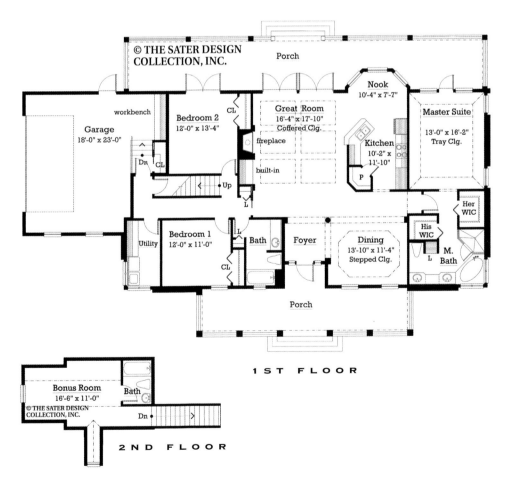

CRESCENT SOMER | 7044

Repeating arches that line the front porch serve as a dramatic prelude to the arched window dormer and twin louvered dormers above. This floor plan opens out to a massive back porch with four different sets of glass doors. The kitchen affords easy access to the dining, nook and great rooms. His-and-hers walk-in closets and a spacious master bath enhance the private master suite.

3 Bedroom / **2** Bath

Living Area: **1,989** sq ft

Bonus Room: **274** sq ft

Width: **81'0"**

Depth: **50'0"**

Exterior Walls: **2x6**

Foundation: crawl space/
opt. basement

Price Code: **C1**

© THE SATER DESIGN COLLECTION, INC.

Porch

workbench

Garage
18'-0" x 23'-0"

Bedroom 2
12'-0" x 13'-4"

CL

Great Room
16'-4" x 17'-10"
Coffered Clg.

fireplace

built-in

Nook
10'-4" x 7'-7"

Kitchen
10'-2" x 11'-10"

Master Suite
13'-0" x 16'-2"
Tray Clg.

Dn

CL

Up

L

Her
WIC

Utility

Bedroom 1
12'-0" x 11'-0"

L

Bath

Foyer

Dining
13'-10" x 11'-4"
Stepped Clg.

His
WIC

M.
Bath

CL

L

Porch

1ST FLOOR

Bonus Room
16'-6" x 11'-0"

Bath

© THE SATER DESIGN
COLLECTION, INC.

Dn

2ND FLOOR

© THE SATER DESIGN COLLECTION, INC.

REAR ELEVATION

7047 | NADINE

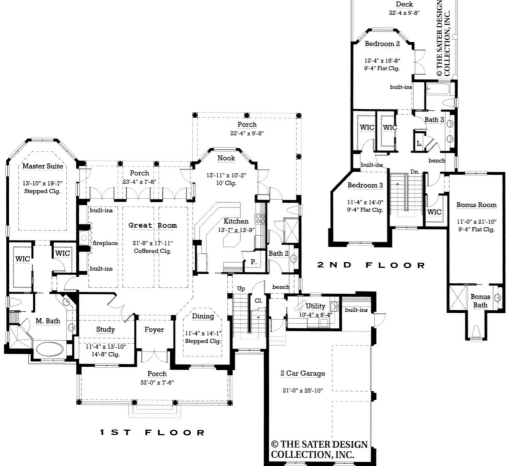

1ST FLOOR

2ND FLOOR

Master Suite
13'-10" x 19'-7"
Stepped Clg.

Porch
23'-4" x 7'-6"

Porch
22'-4" x 9'-8"

Nook
12'-11" x 10'-2"
10' Clg.

built-ins

Great Room
21'-8" x 17'-11"
Coffered Clg.

fireplace

built-ins

Kitchen
13'-7" x 13'-9"

WIC

WIC

Bath 2

M. Bath

Study
11'-4" x 13'-10"
14'-8" Clg.

Foyer

Dining
11'-4" x 14'-1"
Stepped Clg.

Up

Cl.

Utility
10'-4" x 6'-4"

built-ins

bench

Porch
32'-0" x 7'-6"

2 Car Garage
21'-0" x 25'-10"

Deck
22'-4" x 9'-8"

Bedroom 2
12'-4" x 15'-8"
9'-4" Flat Clg.

built-ins

WIC

WIC

Bath 3

L.

built-ins

bench

Bedroom 3
11'-4" x 14'-0"
9'-4" Flat Clg.

Dn.

WIC

Bonus Room
11'-0" x 21'-10"
9'-4" Flat Clg.

Bonus Bath

© THE SATER DESIGN COLLECTION, INC.

Gorgeous sunburst arched windows and detailed fretwork reveal the elegance of French Country-style. Past the foyer, the spacious great room accesses the back porch through three sets of French doors. The kitchen boasts a wraparound eating bar and easy, open entry to the nook and formal dining room. A large study with built-ins, private master suite and ample living area on the upper level add to the design's appeal.

3 Bedroom / **3** Bath

1st Floor: **2,215** sq ft

2nd Floor: **708** sq ft

Living Area: **2,923** sq ft

Bonus Room: **420** sq ft

Width: **75'4"**

Depth: **69'10"**

Exterior Walls: **2x6**

Foundation: crawl space/opt. basement

Price Code: **C3**

REAR ELEVATION

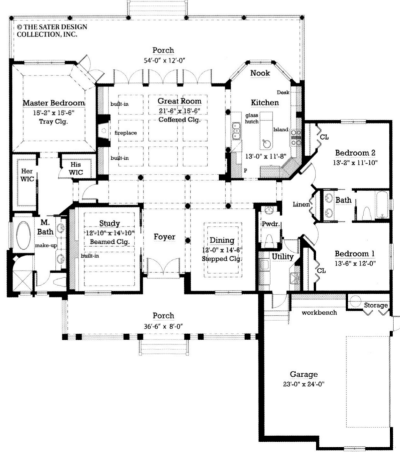

LUNDEN VALLEY | 7050

An impressive gable supplies the focal point for this charming façade. Lunden Valley is an especially open floor plan with large dining, kitchen and great rooms divided by columns. Three sets of French doors open the great room to the back porch; another set is found in the master bedroom. This split floor plan affords easy privacy for the master suite and two secondary bedrooms.

3 Bedroom / **2-1/2** Bath

Living Area: **2,555** sq ft

Width: **70'6"**

Depth: **76'6"**

Exterior Walls: **2x6**

Foundation: crawl space

Price Code: **C3**

© THE SATER DESIGN COLLECTION, INC.

7053 | SARGENT

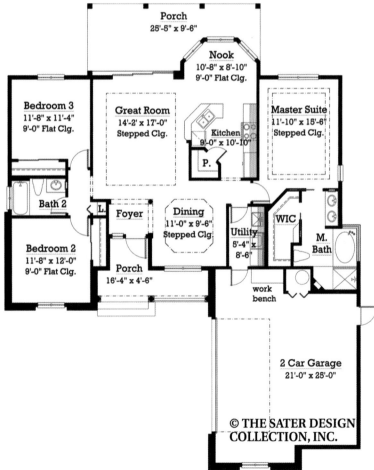

Porch
25'-5" x 9'-6"

Nook
10'-8" x 8'-10"
9'-0" Flat Clg.

Bedroom 3
11'-8" x 11'-4"
9'-0" Flat Clg.

Great Room
14'-2' x 17'-0"
Stepped Clg.

Kitchen
9'-0" x 10'-10"

Master Suite
11'-10" x 15'-6"
Stepped Clg.

P.

Bath 2

L.

Foyer

Dining
11'-0" x 9'-6"
Stepped Clg.

Utility
5'-4" x
8'-6"

WIC

M. Bath

Bedroom 2
11'-8" x 12'-0"
9'-0" Flat Clg.

Porch
16'-4" x 4'-6"

work bench

2 Car Garage
21'-0" x 25'-0"

© THE SATER DESIGN
COLLECTION, INC.

An inviting front porch and multiple gables are found in the simple, rustic design of Sargent. The open floor plan, combined with stepped ceilings, presents the overall living area as generous and inviting. The kitchen includes a convenient eating bar and open access to the nook, dining and great rooms. The private master suite with walk-in closet and large bath are separated from two other secondary bedrooms.

3 Bedroom / **2** Bath

Living Area: **1,487** sq ft

Width: **52'6"**

Depth: **66'0"**

Exterior Walls: **2x6**

Foundation: crawl space

Price Code: **A4**

© THE SATER DESIGN COLLECTION, INC.

REAR ELEVATION

THORNEBURY | 7056

An abundance of sunburst windows and the Old-World charm of a gazebo-style porch make for an unforgettable first impression of Thornebury. Inside, the grand radius staircase and open ceiling to the second floor reveal ample light, views and impressive details. A formal dining room connects via butler's pantry to the gourmet kitchen, and the large, open floor plan features a big leisure room and private master suite with separate foyer.

4 Bedroom / **3-1/2** Bath

1st Floor: **2,083** sq ft

2nd Floor: **1,013** sq ft

Living Area: **3,096** sq ft

Width: **74'0"**

Depth: **88'0"**

Exterior Walls: **2x6**

Foundation: crawl space

Price Code: **C4**

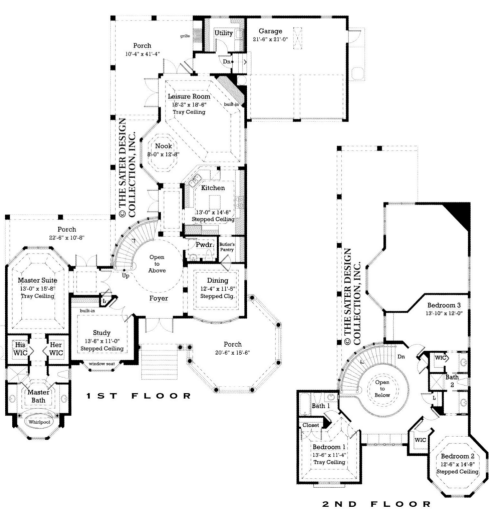

© THE SATER DESIGN COLLECTION, INC.

Porch 10'-4" x 41'-4"

Utility

Garage 21'-6" x 21'-0"

grille

Dn

Leisure Room 18'-2" x 18'-6" Tray Ceiling

built-in

Nook 8'-0" x 12'-8"

Kitchen 13'-0" x 14'-6" Stepped Ceiling

Pwdr.

Butler's Pantry

Porch 22'-6" x 10'-8"

Open to Above

Up

Foyer

Dining 12'-4" x 11'-5" Stepped Clg.

Master Suite 13'-0" x 15'-8" Tray Ceiling

built-in

His WIC

Her WIC

Study 13'-6" x 11'-0" Stepped Ceiling

window seat

Porch 20'-6" x 15'-6"

Master Bath

Whirlpool

1ST FLOOR

Bedroom 3 13'-10" x 12'-0"

Dn

WIC

Bath 2

Open to Below

Bath 1

Closet

Bedroom 1 13'-6" x 11'-4" Tray Ceiling

WIC

Bedroom 2 12'-6" x 14'-9" Stepped Ceiling

2ND FLOOR

© THE SATER DESIGN COLLECTION, INC.

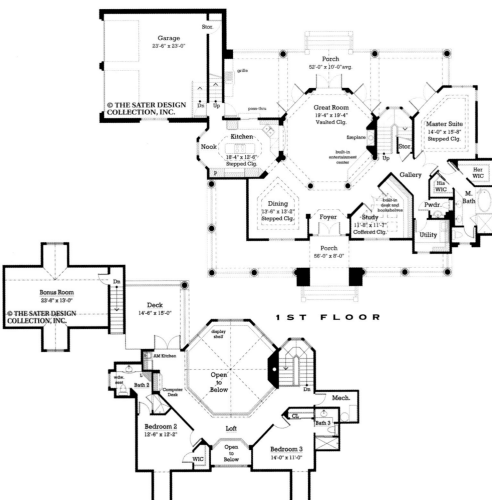

Garage 23'-6" x 23'-0"

Stor.

grille

pass-thru

Dn Up

Porch 52'-0" x 10'-0" avg.

Great Room 19'-4" x 19'-4" Vaulted Clg.

fireplace

built-in entertainment center

Up

Stor.

Master Suite 14'-0" x 15'-8" Stepped Clg.

Her WIC

His WIC

M. Bath

Pwdr.

Kitchen 18'-4" x 12'-6" Stepped Clg.

Nook

P

Dining 13'-6" x 13'-2" Stepped Clg.

Foyer

Study 11'-8" x 11'-7" Coffered Clg.

built-in desk and bookshelves

Gallery

Utility

Porch 56'-0" x 8'-0"

1ST FLOOR

Bonus Room 23'-6" x 13'-0"

Dn

Deck 14'-6" x 15'-0"

AM Kitchen

wdw. seat

Bath 2

Computer Desk

display shelf

Open to Below

Dn

Mech.

Bedroom 2 12'-6" x 12'-2"

WIC

Loft

Open to Below

CL.

Bath 3

Bedroom 3 14'-0" x 11'-0"

2ND FLOOR

7059 | **NEWBERRY**

The sunburst transom surrounded by the stone entry adds a sense of timeless beauty to Newberry. A generous, octagonal-shaped great room with fireplace and three sets of French doors to the back porch centers this large, open floor plan. A formal dining room and gourmet kitchen with pass-thru to the back porch make entertaining easy. A handsome study, private master suite, two guest bedrooms and a bonus room add to the appeal.

3 Bedroom / **3-1/2** Bath

1st Floor: **1,995** sq ft

2nd Floor: **948** sq ft

Living Area: **2,943** sq ft

Bonus Room: **371** sq ft

Width: **90'6"**

Depth: **61'0"**

Exterior Walls: **2x6**

Foundation: crawl space/opt. basement

Price Code: **C3**

© THE SATER DESIGN COLLECTION, INC.

REAR ELEVATION

SANDUSKY | 7062

Style and elegance are found in Sandusky's window dormers, mirrored stone chimneys and split-shake tile roof. A big, welcoming great room — with multiple sets of French doors — features built-ins and open access to the kitchen and nook. Double doors access the master retreat, which also reveals private access to the study. Upstairs, two guest bedrooms, each with large baths and walk-in closets, adjoin the bonus room.

3 Bedroom / **3-1/2** Bath

1st Floor: **2,138** sq ft

2nd Floor: **1,249** sq ft

Living Area: **3,387** sq ft

Width: **77'8"**

Depth: **64'0"**

Exterior Walls: **2x6**

Foundation: crawl space/opt. basement

Price Code: **C4**

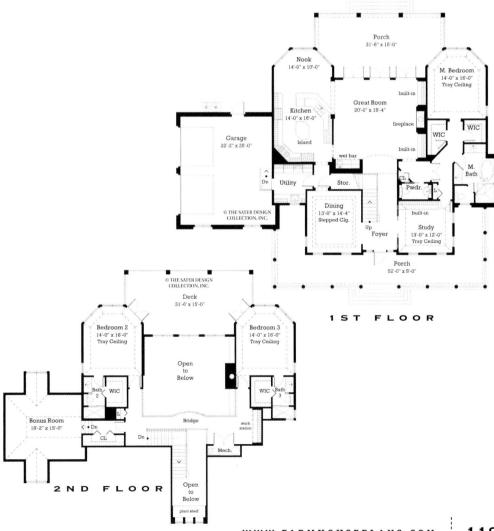

1ST FLOOR

2ND FLOOR

© THE SATER DESIGN COLLECTION, INC.

7068 | KENSETT

Feel the timeless allure of the classic columns, arch-topped dormers and decorative fretwork of Kensett. Inside, stepped and tray ceilings define this open, bright floor plan that features a private master suite with luxury bath; generous dining and great rooms with multiple sets of French doors to the back porch; kitchen with useful eating bar; and, above the garage, a bonus room offering many possible options.

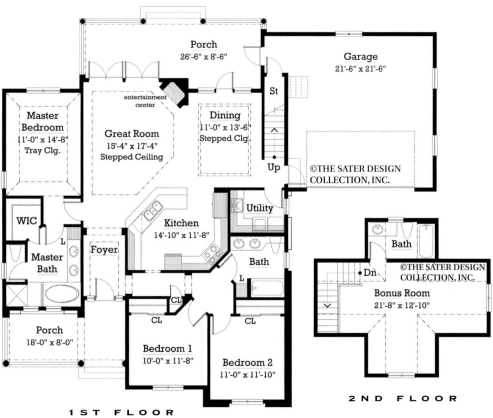

1ST FLOOR

Porch
26'-6" x 8'-6"

Garage
21'-6" x 21'-6"

entertainment center

Master Bedroom
11'-0" x 14'-8"
Tray Clg.

Great Room
15'-4" x 17'-4"
Stepped Ceiling

Dining
11'-0" x 13'-6"
Stepped Clg.

St

Up

©THE SATER DESIGN COLLECTION, INC.

WIC

Master Bath

Foyer

Kitchen
14'-10" x 11'-8"

Utility

Bath

CL

Porch
18'-0" x 8'-0"

CL

Bedroom 1
10'-0" x 11'-8"

Bedroom 2
11'-0" x 11'-10"

CL

2ND FLOOR

Bath

Dn

©THE SATER DESIGN COLLECTION, INC.

Bonus Room
21'-8" x 12'-10"

3 Bedroom / **2** Bath

Living Area: **1,616** sq ft

Bonus Room: **362** sq ft

Width: **64'0"**

Depth: **55'0"**

Exterior Walls: **2x6**

Foundation: crawl space

Price Code: **C1**

© THE SATER DESIGN COLLECTION, INC.

REAR ELEVATION

DAVENPORT | 7074

Davenport's detailed trim work, clapboard siding and stonework make for a façade with Old-World appeal. The foyer unfolds into the dining and great rooms, with instant views to the back porch. The master suite also opens to the back porch through French doors. A gourmet kitchen features a pass-thru to the great room, and a bonus room over the garage offers even more opportunities to expand your living space.

3 Bedroom / **2** Bath

Living Area: **1,526** sq ft

Bonus Room: **336** sq ft

Width: **65'0"**

Depth: **54'0"**

Exterior Walls: **2x6**

Foundation: crawl space

Price Code: **C1**

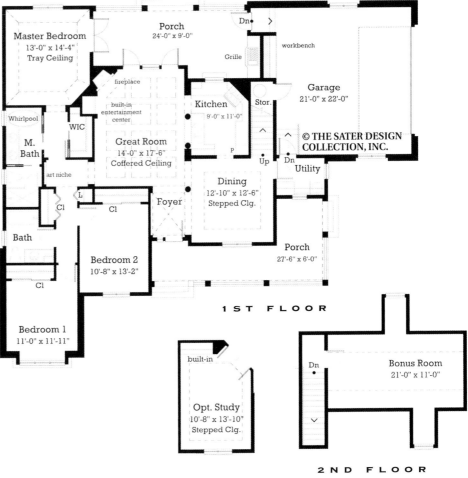

Master Bedroom
13'-0" x 14'-4"
Tray Ceiling

Porch
24'-0" x 9'-0"

Dn

workbench

Grille

fireplace

built-in entertainment center

Whirlpool

WIC

M. Bath

Kitchen
9'-0" x 11'-0"

Stor.

Garage
21'-0" x 22'-0"

© THE SATER DESIGN COLLECTION, INC.

Great Room
14'-0" x 17'-6"
Coffered Ceiling

Up

Dn

Utility

art niche

Cl

Cl

L

Foyer

Dining
12'-10" x 12'-6"
Stepped Clg.

Bath

Cl

Bedroom 2
10'-8" x 13'-2"

Porch
27'-6" x 6'-0"

Bedroom 1
11'-0" x 11'-11"

1ST FLOOR

built-in

Opt. Study
10'-8" x 13'-10"
Stepped Clg.

Dn

Bonus Room
21'-0" x 11'-0"

2ND FLOOR

Victorian Country

For a number of reasons, a Victorian home's sensibility can be described by the word "freedom". Freedom from symmetrical façades and box-like shapes; freedom from the usual, the unadorned and plain. Victorian style is marked by a great sense of change and growth — and a newness emerges, an affinity for both formal and casual touches that are designed to be textured, bold and elaborate. These Victorian Country homes are a feast for the eyes — detailed trim; finely crafted fish-scale siding and arch-top windows; ornate fixtures, balustrades, fretwork and more that will capture your attention. And the appeal only grows when you find interiors designed with roomy, private floor plans; impressive, multiple ceiling treatments; formal dining rooms and open, inviting kitchens; private decks, quiet sitting rooms, and spacious, unique bedroom suites. Discover the detailed finery of these Victorian Country designs and excite your senses with the sights and qualities of a distinctive era.

REAR ELEVATION

ALEXANDRE 6849

Fish-scale siding, an expansive porch and a wealth of arched windows make for an amazing first impression. Inside, the grand radius staircase and open ceiling to the second floor reveal ample light, views and impressive details. A formal dining room connects via butler's pantry to the gourmet kitchen, and the open floor plan features a leisure room and private master suite with foyer.

4 Bedroom / **3-1/2** Bath

1st Floor: **2,083** sq ft

2nd Floor: **1,013** sq ft

Living Area: **3,096** sq ft

Width: **74'0"**

Depth: **88'0"**

Exterior Walls: **2x6**

Foundation: crawl space

Price Code: **C4**

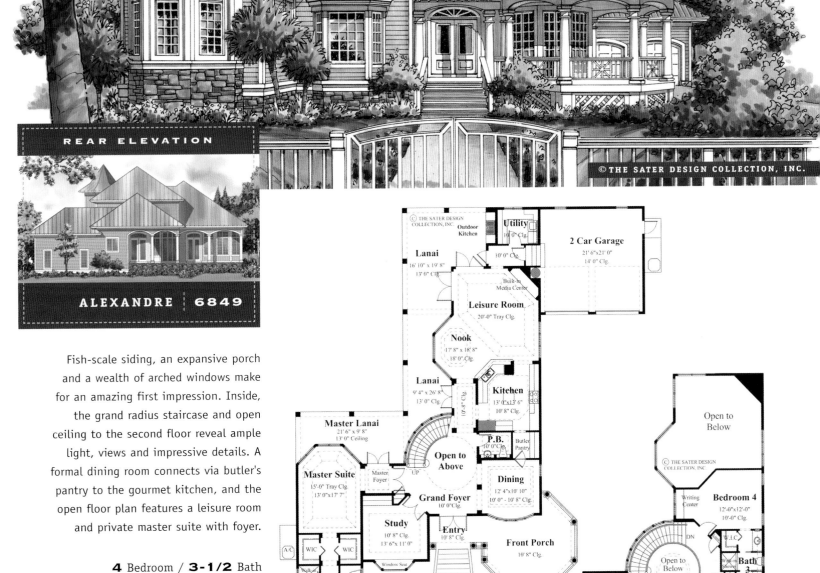

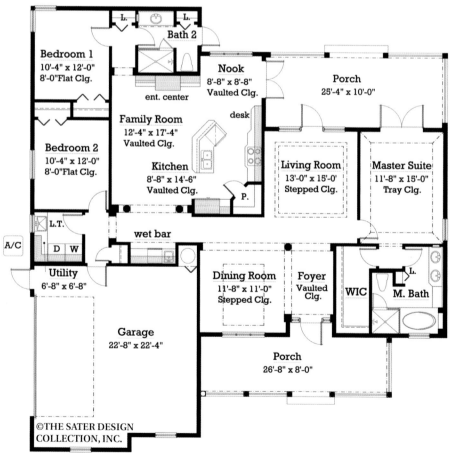

Bath 2

Bedroom 1
10'-4" x 12'-0"
8'-0"Flat Clg.

Nook
8'-8" x 8'-8"
Vaulted Clg.

ent. center

Porch
25'-4" x 10'-0"

desk

Family Room
12'-4" x 17'-4"
Vaulted Clg.

Bedroom 2
10'-4" x 12'-0"
8'-0"Flat Clg.

Kitchen
8'-8" x 14'-6"
Vaulted Clg.

Living Room
13'-0" x 15'-0"
Stepped Clg.

Master Suite
11'-8" x 15'-0"
Tray Clg.

A/C

D   W

L.T.

wet bar

P.

Utility
6'-8" x 6'-8"

Dining Room
11'-8" x 11'-0"
Stepped Clg.

Foyer
Vaulted
Clg.

WIC

M. Bath

L.

Garage
22'-8" x 22'-4"

Porch
26'-8" x 8'-0"

REAR ELEVATION

7003 | MALLARD RIDGE

Decorative vents and fish-scale trim are just a few of the charming details to be found in Mallard Ridge. This roomy floor plan features an open kitchen with large pantry and nook, and the family room is flanked by a wet bar and built-in entertainment center. A huge walk-in closet and master bath, along with French doors to the back porch, make for an impressive and private master suite.

3 Bedroom / **2** Bath

Living Area: **1,848** sq ft

Width: **58'0"**

Depth: **59'6"**

Exterior Walls: **2x6**

Foundation: crawl space

Price Code: **C1**

REAR ELEVATION

VILLETTE | 7006

Decorative fretwork adorns the exterior of Villette, as well as a front porch with deep-cut trim work. Inside, more columns and coffered ceilings provide understated elegance in the living and dining rooms. With its handy pass-thru to the dining room, the kitchen also features a walk-in pantry and spacious nook. Enjoy the view through a wall of windows from the office or exit the generous master suite through French doors.

3 Bedroom / **2** Bath

Living Area: **2,487** sq ft

Width: **70'0"**

Depth: **72'0"**

Exterior Walls: **2x6**

Foundation: slab/ opt. basement

Price Code: **C2**

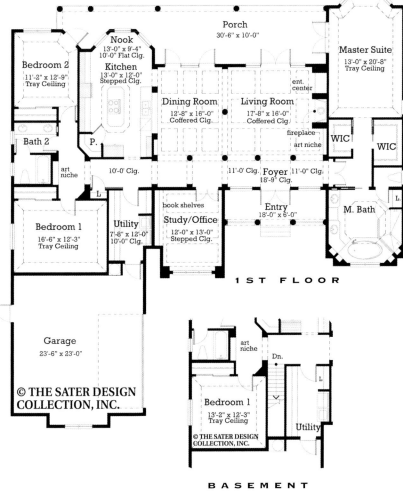

1ST FLOOR

Porch
30'-6" x 10'-0"

Nook
13'-0" x 9'-4"
10'-0" Flat Clg.

Kitchen
13'-0" x 12'-0"
Stepped Clg.

Bedroom 2
11'-2" x 12'-9"
Tray Ceiling

Master Suite
13'-0" x 20'-8"
Tray Ceiling

Dining Room
12'-8" x 16'-0"
Coffered Clg.

Living Room
17'-8" x 16'-0"
Coffered Clg.

ent. center

Bath 2

P.

fireplace
art niche

WIC

WIC

art niche

10'-0" Clg.

11'-0" Clg.

Foyer
18'-9" Clg.

11'-0" Clg.

M. Bath

book shelves

Entry
18'-0" x 6'-0"

Bedroom 1
16'-6" x 12'-3"
Tray Ceiling

Utility
7'-8" x 12'-0"
10'-0" Clg.

Study/Office
12'-0" x 13'-0"
Stepped Clg.

Garage
23'-6" x 23'-0"

art niche

Dn.

Bedroom 1
13'-2" x 12'-3"
Tray Ceiling

Utility

BASEMENT STAIR OPTION

© THE SATER DESIGN COLLECTION, INC.

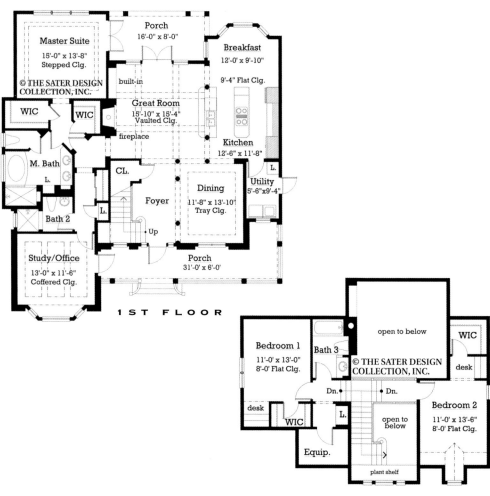

1ST FLOOR

- Master Suite — 15'-0" x 13'-8" Stepped Clg.
- © THE SATER DESIGN COLLECTION, INC.
- WIC
- WIC
- M. Bath
- Bath 2
- Study/Office — 13'-0" x 11'-6" Coffered Clg.
- Porch — 16'-0" x 8'-0"
- built-in
- Great Room — 15'-10" x 15'-4" Vaulted Clg.
- fireplace
- CL.
- Foyer
- Dining — 11'-8" x 13'-10" Tray Clg.
- Up
- Porch — 31'-0' x 6'-0'
- Breakfast — 12'-0' x 9'-10"
- 9'-4" Flat Clg.
- Kitchen — 12'-6" x 11'-8"
- Utility — 5'-6"x9'-4"
- L.

2ND FLOOR

- Bedroom 1 — 11'-0' x 13'-0" 8'-0' Flat Clg.
- Bath 3
- open to below
- WIC
- desk
- desk
- © THE SATER DESIGN COLLECTION, INC.
- Dn.
- Dn.
- L.
- WIC
- open to below
- Bedroom 2 — 11'-0' x 13'-6" 8'-0' Flat Clg.
- Equip.
- plant shelf

REAR ELEVATION

7009 | LA ROUX

Old-World charm is everywhere in La Roux — from the dormer windows to the decorative fretwork and pickets. The plan's centerpiece — an impressive, open great room — features a fireplace, built-in cabinetry and French doors under a vaulted beamed ceiling. A pair of spare bedrooms feature built-in desks and walk-in closets. A stepped ceiling, double walk-in closets and a lavish bath complement the master suite.

3 Bedroom / **3** Bath

1st Floor: **1,710** sq ft

2nd Floor: **618** sq ft

Living Area: **2,328** sq ft

Width: **47'0"**

Depth: **50'0"**

Exterior Walls: **2x6**

Foundation: crawl space/ opt. basement

Price Code: **C2**

© THE SATER DESIGN COLLECTION, INC

REAR ELEVATION

MAGNOLIA | 7012

Charm is detailed throughout Magnolia's façade with fish-scale siding, arch-top windows and decorative shutters and dormers. This open, airy plan features a vaulted ceiling in the living room as well as built-in cabinetry, a fireplace and retreating glass doors. The breakfast nook and master suite both open up to the back porch, and the plan's study could easily function as a fourth bedroom.

3 Bedroom / **2** Bath

Living Area: **1,822** sq ft

Width: **58'0"**

Depth: **66'8"**

Exterior Walls: **2x6**

Foundation: basement

Price Code: **C1**

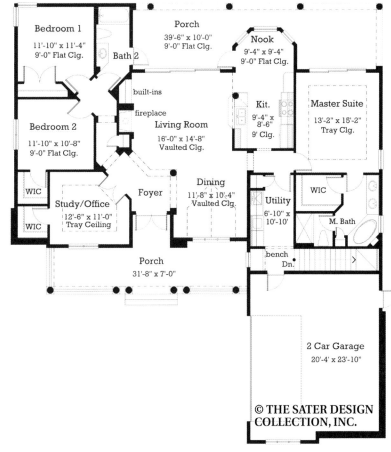

Bedroom 1
11'-10" x 11'-4"
9'-0" Flat Clg.

Bath 2

Porch
39'-6" x 10'-0"
9'-0" Flat Clg.

Nook
9'-4" x 9'-4"
9'-0" Flat Clg.

built-ins

fireplace

Kit.
9'-4" x
8'-6"
9' Clg.

Master Suite
13'-2" x 15'-2"
Tray Clg.

Bedroom 2
11'-10" x 10'-8"
9'-0" Flat Clg.

Living Room
16'-0" x 14'-8"
Vaulted Clg.

WIC

WIC

Foyer

Dining
11'-8" x 10'-4"
Vaulted Clg.

Utility
6'-10" x
10'-10'

WIC

M. Bath

WIC

Study/Office
12'-6" x 11'-0"
Tray Ceiling

bench
Dn.

Porch
31'-8" x 7'-0"

2 Car Garage
20'-4' x 23'-10"

© THE SATER DESIGN
COLLECTION, INC.

© THE SATER DESIGN COLLECTION, INC.

REAR ELEVATION

7015 | HUNTINGTON

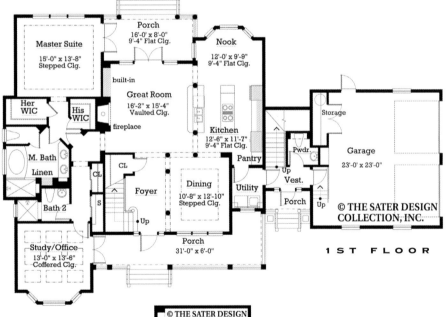

1ST FLOOR

Master Suite
15'-0" x 13'-8"
Stepped Clg.

Porch
16'-0" x 8'-0"
9'-4" Flat Clg.

Nook
12'-0" x 9'-9"
9'-4" Flat Clg.

built-in

Great Room
16'-2" x 15'-4"
Vaulted Clg.

Her WIC

His WIC

fireplace

Kitchen
12'-6" x 11'-7"
9'-4" Flat Clg.

Storage

M. Bath

Linen

CL

Foyer

Dining
10'-8" x 12'-10"
Stepped Clg.

Pantry

Utility

Powder

Up Vest.

Porch

Up

Garage
23'-0" x 23'-0"

Bath 2

CL

S

© THE SATER DESIGN COLLECTION, INC.

Study/Office
13'-0" x 13'-6"
Coffered Clg.

Up

Porch
31'-0" x 6'-0"

2ND FLOOR

© THE SATER DESIGN COLLECTION, INC.

open to below

Bedroom 1
11'-0" x 17'-0"
8'-0" Flat Clg.

WIC

Storage

Bath 4

Equip.

WIC

Dn.

Bonus Room
23'-0" x 12'-0"
Vaulted Clg.

bridge

Dn.

Dn.

Bath 3

Bedroom 2
11'-0" x 13'-4"
8'-0" Flat Clg.

open to below

plant shelf

Decorative details abound in Huntington where square columns, classic fretwork and balustrades draw together the essence of grace. This open, expansive floor plan offers elegant columns, built-in cabinetry, kitchen work island and pass-thru and even a bonus room with separate entry. A secluded master suite, pampering master bath and multiple sets of French doors throughout add to the appeal.

3 Bedroom / **4-1/2** Bath

1st Floor: **1,834** sq ft

2nd Floor: **732** sq ft

Living Area: **2,566** sq ft

Bonus Room: **379** sq ft

Width: **79'0"**

Depth: **50'0"**

Exterior Walls: **2x6**

Foundation: crawl space/opt. basement

Price Code: **C3**

REAR ELEVATION

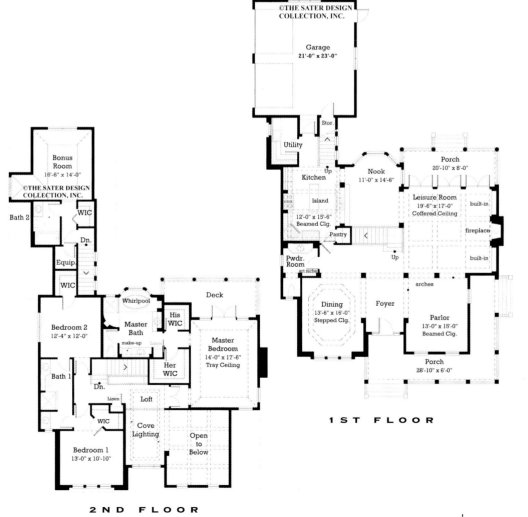

MARAVELLA | 7018

Maravella's exquisite pediment, columns and Palladian windows only begin to describe this home's attention to detail. Arches, columns and ceiling treatments define the living space throughout the plan. The leisure room boasts three sets of French doors opening to the back porch and the master suite features its own private deck. Built-ins, spacious walk-ins and a large, accessible kitchen add to the appeal.

3 Bedroom / **2-1/2** Bath

1st Floor: **1,642** sq ft

2nd Floor: **1,205** sq ft

Living Area: **2,847** sq ft

Bonus Room: **340** sq ft

Width: **53'7"**

Depth: **72'6"**

Exterior Walls: **2x6**

Foundation: crawl space

Price Code: **C3**

© THE SATER DESIGN COLLECTION, INC.

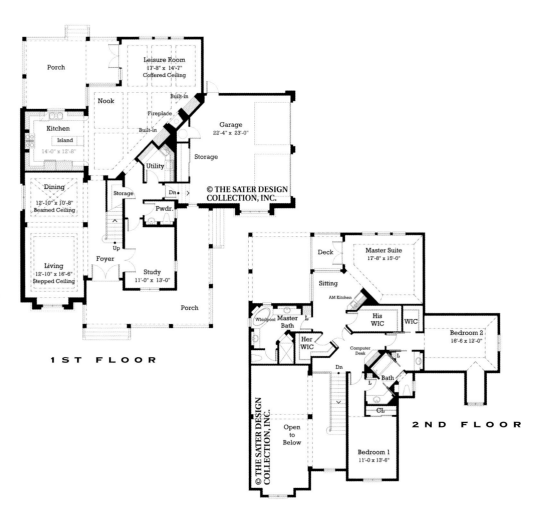

REAR ELEVATION

7021 | REMY COURT

Victorian fish-scale siding, decorative fretwork and corbels provide Remy Court with equal parts charm and character. Inside, the uniquely designed open kitchen, nook and leisure room create a massive living space with built-ins, fireplace and a beamed coffered ceiling treatment. The secluded master suite features a private deck, dual walk-in closets and an impressive sitting area. Two secondary bedrooms share a bath and built-in computer desk.

3 Bedroom / **2-1/2** Bath

1st Floor: **1,664** sq ft

2nd Floor: **1,471** sq ft

Living Area: **3,135** sq ft

Width: **60'10"**

Depth: **62'0"**

Exterior Walls: **2x6**

Foundation: crawl space/ opt. basement

Price Code: **C4**

© THE SATER DESIGN COLLECTION, INC.

REAR ELEVATION

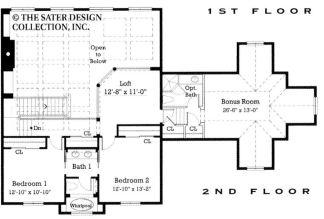

GEORGETTE | 7024

The louvered shutters, decorative corbels and distinctive widow's walk feel like a welcome step back in time. The unique and spacious interior creates an open, inviting environment through a large loft, open kitchen and great room with French doors that expand your living area outward. Find new options with the unique bonus room and the private foyer and spacious bath in the master retreat.

3 Bedroom / **2-1/2** Bath

1st Floor: **2,151** sq ft

2nd Floor: **734** sq ft

Living Area: **2,885** sq ft

Bonus Room: **522** sq ft

Width: **99'0"**

Depth: **56'0"**

Exterior Walls: **2x6**

Foundation: crawl space/opt. basement

Price Code: **C3**

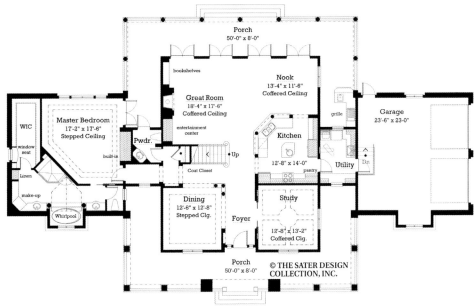

1ST FLOOR

2ND FLOOR

© THE SATER DESIGN COLLECTION, INC.

7027 | ASHLEY

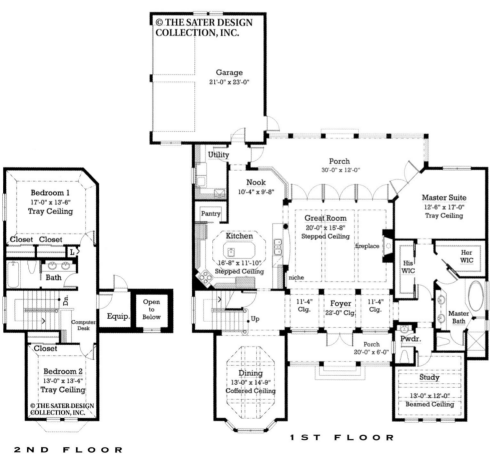

© THE SATER DESIGN COLLECTION, INC.

2ND FLOOR

Bedroom 1
17'-0" x 13'-6"
Tray Ceiling

Closet | Closet

Bath

Computer Desk

Closet

Bedroom 2
13'-0" x 13'-4"
Tray Ceiling

© THE SATER DESIGN COLLECTION, INC.

Dn.

Equip. | Open to Below

Garage
21'-0" x 23'-0"

Utility

Nook
10'-4" x 9'-8"

Pantry

Porch
30'-0" x 12'-0"

Kitchen
16'-8" x 11'-10"
Stepped Ceiling

Great Room
20'-0" x 15'-8"
Stepped Ceiling

fireplace

niche

Master Suite
12'-6" x 17'-0"
Tray Ceiling

His WIC

Her WIC

Master Bath

11'-4" Clg. | Foyer 22'-0" Clg. | 11'-4" Clg.

Up

Porch
20'-0" x 6'-0"

Pwdr.

Dining
13'-0" x 14'-9"
Coffered Ceiling

Study
13'-0" x 12'-0"
Beamed Ceiling

1ST FLOOR

Enjoy elaborate detail in the fish-scale siding, arch-top windows and an impressive central dormer window. The open, engaging living space features columns lining the foyer, a sizeable kitchen with walk-in pantry, and a great room boasting a fireplace and art niche. The secluded master retreat is complete with a luxurious bath and French-door access to the back porch. Upstairs, two secondary bedrooms enjoy a built-in desk and cabinetry.

3 Bedroom / **2-1/2** Bath

1st Floor: **2,073** sq ft

2nd Floor: **682** sq ft

Living Area: **2,755** sq ft

Width: **64'0"**

Depth: **76'2"**

Exterior Walls: **2x6**

Foundation: crawl space/ opt. basement

Price Code: **C3**

© THE SATER DESIGN COLLECTION, INC.

REAR ELEVATION

ORLINA | 7030

The Orlina invites you to take it all in — decorative fretwork, the striking center pediment, fish-scale siding and corbels. The open, formal living and dining rooms feature stepped and beamed ceilings and the large kitchen with work island opens wide into the nook and leisure room. Two big bedrooms, an impressive sitting room, a magnificent master suite and even a bonus room are discovered upstairs.

3 Bedroom / **2-1/2** Bath

1st Floor: **1,387** sq ft

2nd Floor: **1,175** sq ft

Living Area: **2,562** sq ft

Bonus Room: **362** sq ft

Width: **54'6"**

Depth: **78'6"**

Exterior Walls: **2x6**

Foundation: crawl space

Price Code: **C3**

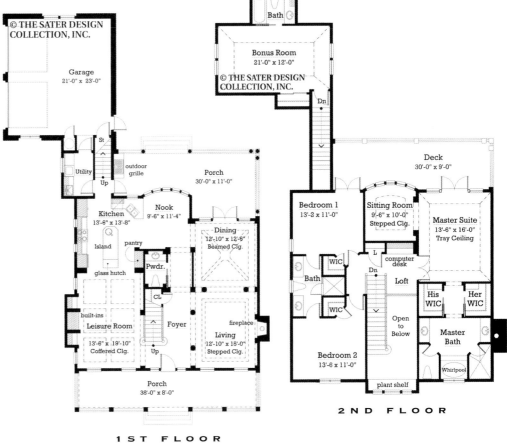

© THE SATER DESIGN COLLECTION, INC.

Garage
21'-0" x 23'-0"

Utility

St

Up

outdoor grille

Porch
30'-0" x 11'-0"

Nook
9'-6" x 11'-4"

Kitchen
13'-6" x 13'-8"

Island

pantry

glass hutch

Pwdr.

CL

Dining
12'-10" x 12'-6"
Beamed Clg.

built-ins

Leisure Room
13'-6" x 19'-10"
Coffered Clg.

Foyer

Up

fireplace

Living
12'-10" x 15'-0"
Stepped Clg.

Porch
38'-0" x 8'-0"

1ST FLOOR

Bath

Bonus Room
21'-0" x 12'-0"

© THE SATER DESIGN COLLECTION, INC.

Dn

Deck
30'-0" x 9'-0"

Bedroom 1
13'-2 x 11'-0"

Sitting Room
9'-6" x 10'-0"
Stepped Clg.

Master Suite
13'-6" x 16'-0"
Tray Ceiling

WIC

Bath

L

computer desk

Dn

Loft

His WIC

Her WIC

WIC

Open to Below

Master Bath

Bedroom 2
13'-6" x 11'-0"

plant shelf

Whirlpool

2ND FLOOR

© THE SATER DESIGN COLLECTION, INC.

REAR ELEVATION

7033 | BRANTLEY PINES

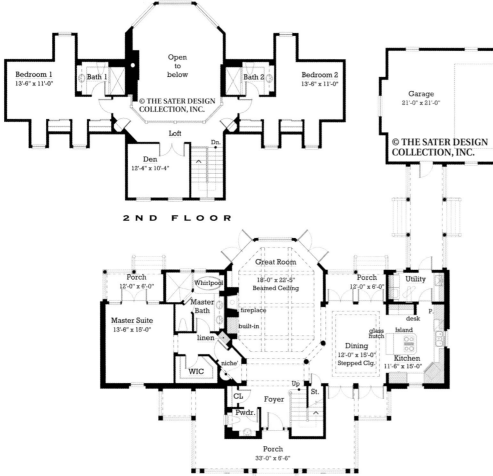

2ND FLOOR

Bedroom 1
13'-6" x 11'-0"

Bath 1

Open to below

© THE SATER DESIGN COLLECTION, INC.

Bath 2

Bedroom 2
13'-6" x 11'-0"

Loft

Dn.

Den
12'-4" x 10'-4"

Garage
21'-0" x 21'-0"

© THE SATER DESIGN COLLECTION, INC.

1ST FLOOR

Porch
12'-0" x 6'-0"

Whirlpool

Great Room
18'-0" x 22'-5"
Beamed Ceiling

Porch
12'-0" x 6'-0"

Utility

Master Bath

fireplace

built-in

Master Suite
13'-6" x 15'-0"

linen

desk

P.

glass hutch

Island

niche

Dining
12'-0" x 15'-0"
Stepped Clg.

Kitchen
11'-6" x 15'-0"

WIC

CL

Foyer

St.

Up

Pwdr.

Porch
33'-0" x 6'-6"

Classic columns, a striking pediment above the porch and center gable give Brantley Pines a sense of Victorian splendor. The eye-catching octagonal great room opens through French doors to the backyard. It is flanked by a formal dining room and open kitchen on one side and an extraordinary master suite with private porch on the other. Secondary bedrooms, a den, loft and more are found upstairs.

3 Bedroom / **3-1/2** Bath

1st Floor: **1,627** sq ft

2nd Floor: **1,024** sq ft

Living Area: **2,651** sq ft

Width: **78'6"**

Depth: **80'6"**

Exterior Walls: **2x6**

Foundation: crawl space/ opt. basement

Price Code: **C3**

© THE SATER DESIGN COLLECTION, INC.

REAR ELEVATION

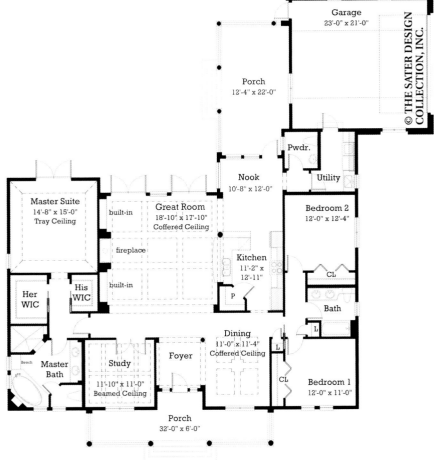

WHITNEY | 7036

Find the beauty in the details of the multi-paned windows, decorative fretwork and prominent center gable of the Whitney façade. Inside, the considerable great room, formal dining room, kitchen and nook all make for an open, flowing quality. A built-in fireplace and cabinetry, multiple sets of French doors, a handsome study and private master suite are all prominently featured.

3 Bedroom / **2-1/2** Bath

Living Area: **2,329** sq ft

Width: **72'0"**

Depth: **73'10"**

Exterior Walls: **2x6**

Foundation: crawl space

Price Code: **C2**

© THE SATER DESIGN COLLECTION, INC.

Garage
23'-0" x 21'-0"

Porch
12'-4" x 22'-0"

Pwdr.

Nook
10'-8" x 12'-0"

Utility

Bedroom 2
12'-0" x 12'-4"

Master Suite
14'-8" x 15'-0"
Tray Ceiling

built-in

Great Room
18'-10" x 17'-10"
Coffered Ceiling

fireplace

Kitchen
11'-2" x 12'-11"

built-in

CL

Her WIC

His WIC

P

Bath

Master Bath

Study
11'-10" x 11'-0"
Beamed Ceiling

Foyer

Dining
11'-0" x 11'-4"
Coffered Ceiling

CL

Bedroom 1
12'-0" x 11'-0"

Bench

Porch
32'-0" x 6'-0"

© THE SATER DESIGN COLLECTION, INC.

REAR ELEVATION

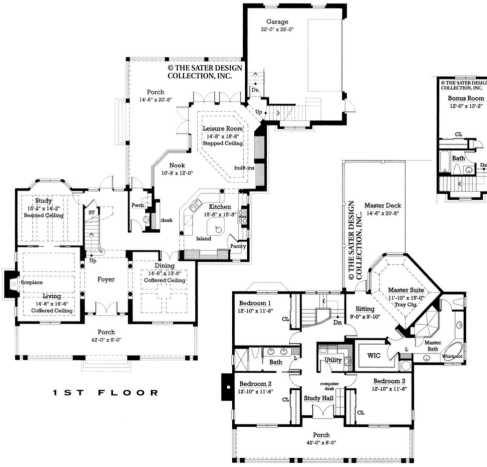

© THE SATER DESIGN COLLECTION, INC.

7039 | CHILTON HILLS

The recessed covered entry, dormers and gables provide Chilton Hills with a warm, welcoming façade. There's a lot to love in this unique design: the efficient, open kitchen with convenient pass-thru; the large leisure room with triple French doors to the back porch; the formal living and dining rooms set off by stately columns; the private upper floor featuring a unique master suite and three secondary bedrooms; and more.

4 Bedroom / **2-1/2** Bath

1st Floor: **1,865** sq ft

2nd Floor: **1,477** sq ft

Living Area: **3,342** sq ft

Bonus Room: **282** sq ft

Width: **79'6"**

Depth: **79'2"**

Exterior Walls: **2x6**

Foundation: crawl space/opt. basement

Price Code: **C4**

1ST FLOOR

2ND FLOOR

© THE SATER DESIGN COLLECTION, INC.

REAR ELEVATION

MEADOWSBROOK 7042

A central gable with matchstick detailing crowns a pair of arch-top dormers, creating a wonderful complement to the wraparound porch's classic columns. This open floor plan features exciting details around every corner including stepped and coffered ceilings, built-in shelves and computer desk, a butler's pantry and an outdoor grill. A pair of secondary bedrooms upstairs also features private decks and walk-in closets.

3 Bedroom / **2-1/2** Bath

1st Floor: **1,493** sq ft

2nd Floor: **676** sq ft

Living Area: **2,169** sq ft

Width: **70'0"**

Depth: **55'8"**

Exterior Walls: **2x6**

Foundation: crawl space/opt. basement

Price Code: **C2**

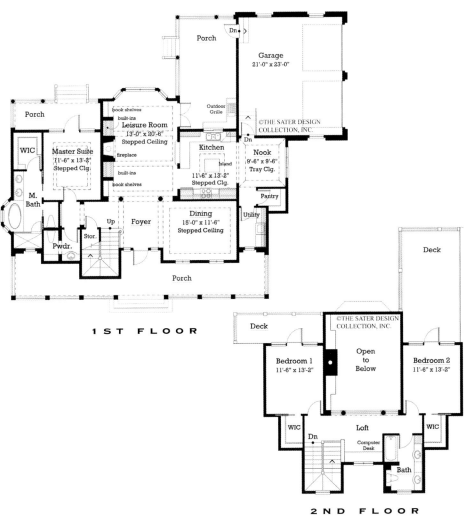

1ST FLOOR

2ND FLOOR

© THE SATER DESIGN COLLECTION, INC.

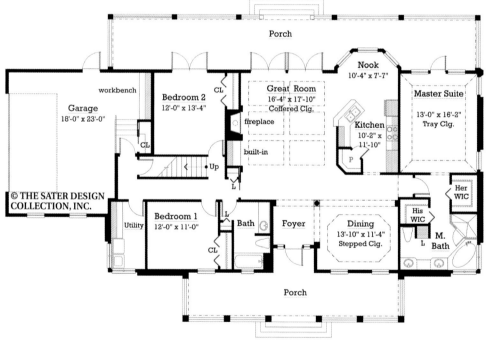

1ST FLOOR

2ND FLOOR

REAR ELEVATION

7045 | SAVILLE

Feel the allure of the Victorian style in Saville's elegant fretwork, balustrades, and sunburst-windowed gable. This floor plan opens out to a generous back porch in four different sets of glass doors, and the kitchen affords easy access to the dining, nook and great rooms. His-and-hers walk-in closets and a spacious master bath feature prominently in the private master suite.

3 Bedroom / **2** Bath

Living Area: **1,989** sq ft

Bonus Room: **274** sq ft

Width: **81'0"**

Depth: **50'0"**

Exterior Walls: **2x6**

Foundation: crawl space/ opt. basement

Price Code: **C1**

© THE SATER DESIGN COLLECTION, INC.

REAR ELEVATION

WILONA | 7048

Classic columns and arch-top windows provide for elegant Victorian design. Past the foyer, the spacious great room accesses the back porch through three sets of French doors. The kitchen boasts a wraparound eating bar and easy, open entry to the nook and formal dining room. A large study with built-ins, private master suite and ample living area on the upper level add to the design's appeal.

3 Bedroom / **3** Bath

1st Floor: **2,215** sq ft

2nd Floor: **708** sq ft

Living Area: **2,923** sq ft

Bonus Room: **420** sq ft

Width: **76'4"**

Depth: **69'10"**

Exterior Walls: **2x6**

Foundation: crawl space/opt. basement

Price Code: **C3**

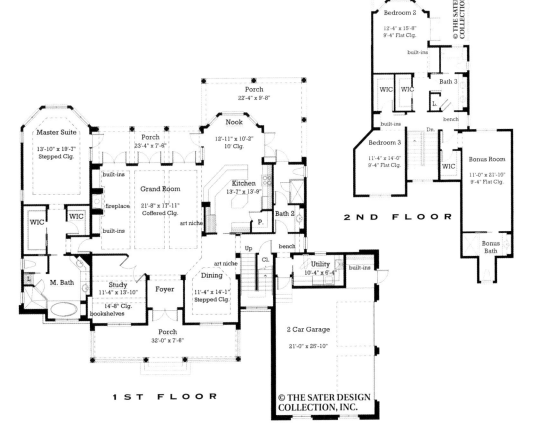

1ST FLOOR

2ND FLOOR

© THE SATER DESIGN COLLECTION, INC.

© THE SATER DESIGN COLLECTION, INC.

REAR ELEVATION

7054 | CASSIDY

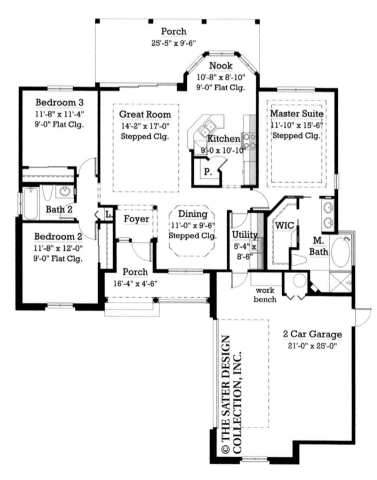

Porch
25'-5" x 9'-6"

Nook
10'-8" x 8'-10"
9'-0" Flat Clg.

Bedroom 3
11'-8" x 11'-4"
9'-0" Flat Clg.

Great Room
14'-2" x 17'-0"
Stepped Clg.

Master Suite
11'-10" x 15'-6"
Stepped Clg.

Kitchen
9'-0 x 10'-10"

P.

Bath 2

L.

Foyer

Dining
11'-0" x 9'-6"
Stepped Clg.

WIC

Bedroom 2
11'-8" x 12'-0"
9'-0" Flat Clg.

Utility
5'-4" x
8'-6"

M. Bath

Porch
16'-4" x 4'-6"

work bench

© THE SATER DESIGN
COLLECTION, INC.

2 Car Garage
21'-0" x 25'-0"

Decorative trim work and fish-scale siding complete the simple, Victorian design of Cassidy. The open floor plan, combined with stepped ceilings, presents the overall living area as generous and inviting. The kitchen includes a convenient eating bar and open access to the nook, dining and great rooms. The private master suite with walk-in closet and large bath is separated from two other secondary bedrooms.

3 Bedroom / **2** Bath

Living Area: **1,487** sq ft

Width: **52'6"**

Depth: **66'0"**

Exterior Walls: **2x6**

Foundation: crawl space

Price Code: **A4**

REAR ELEVATION

CHELSEA | 7057

© THE SATER DESIGN COLLECTION, INC.

The striking turret above the round, expansive porch and a wealth of arched windows make for an amazing first impression of Chelsea. Inside, the grand radius staircase and open ceiling to the second floor reveal ample light, views and impressive details. A formal dining room connects via butler's pantry to the gourmet kitchen, and the large, open floor plan features a big leisure room and private master suite with separate foyer.

4 Bedroom / **3-1/2** Bath

1st Floor: **2,083** sq ft

2nd Floor: **1,013** sq ft

Living Area: **3,096** sq ft

Width: **74'0"**

Depth: **88'6"**

Exterior Walls: **2x6**

Foundation: crawl space

Price Code: **C4**

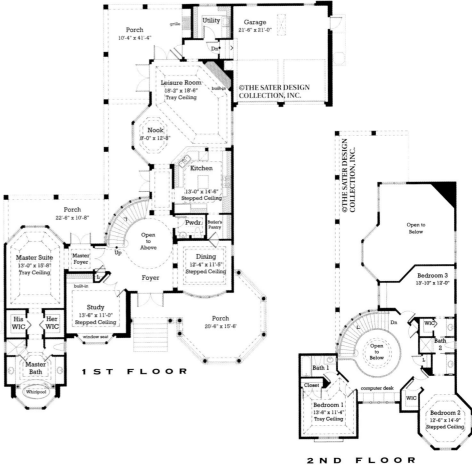

1ST FLOOR

2ND FLOOR

© THE SATER DESIGN COLLECTION, INC.

REAR ELEVATION

7060 | MONROE

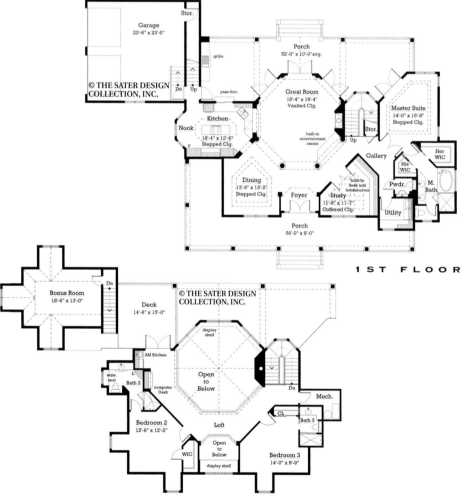

© THE SATER DESIGN COLLECTION, INC.

1ST FLOOR

2ND FLOOR

Fancy fretwork and brick columns create an inviting wraparound porch to welcome guests to Monroe. A generous, octagonal-shaped great room — with fireplace and three sets of French doors to the back porch — centers this large, open floor plan. A formal dining room and gourmet kitchen with pass-thru to the back porch make entertaining easy. A handsome study, private master suite, two guest bedrooms and a bonus room add to the appeal.

3 Bedroom / **3-1/2** Bath

1st Floor: **1,874** sq ft

2nd Floor: **966** sq ft

Living Area: **2,840** sq ft

Bonus Room: **387** sq ft

Width: **90'0"**

Depth: **58'6"**

Exterior Walls: **2x6**

Foundation: crawl space/opt. basement

Price Code: **C3**

REAR ELEVATION

VERNAY | 7063

Enjoy the Victorian touches in Vernay's brick columns and coordinating balustrades and fretwork. The welcoming great room features multiple sets of French doors, built-ins and open access to the kitchen and nook. Double doors access the master retreat, which also reveals private access to the large study. Upstairs, two guest bedrooms, each with large baths and walk-in closets, adjoin a spacious bonus room.

3 Bedroom / **3-1/2** Bath

1st Floor: **2,138** sq ft

2nd Floor: **944** sq ft

Living Area: **3,082** sq ft

Bonus Room: **427** sq ft

Width: **77'2"**

Depth: **64'0"**

Exterior Walls: **2x6**

Foundation: crawl space/opt. basement

Price Code: **C4**

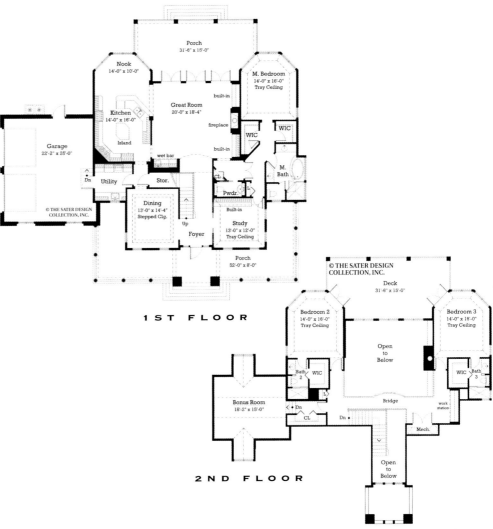

1ST FLOOR

2ND FLOOR

© THE SATER DESIGN COLLECTION, INC.

REAR ELEVATION

7066 | CALANDRE

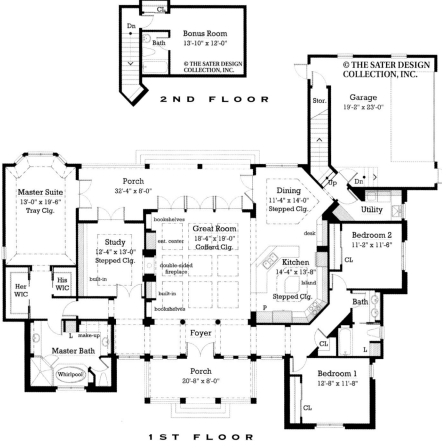

2ND FLOOR

CL.

Dn

Bath

Bonus Room
13'-10" x 12'-0"

© THE SATER DESIGN
COLLECTION, INC.

© THE SATER DESIGN
COLLECTION, INC.

Stor.

Garage
19'-2" x 23'-0"

Up Dn

Dining
11'-4" x 14'-0"
Stepped Clg.

Utility

Master Suite
13'-0" x 19'-6"
Tray Clg.

Porch
32'-4" x 8'-0"

bookshelves

ent. center

Great Room
18'-4" x 19'-0"
Cofferd Clg.

desk

Bedroom 2
11'-2" x 11'-6"

CL

Study
12'-4" x 13'-0"
Stepped Clg.

built-in

double-sided
fireplace

built-in

Kitchen
14'-4" x 13'-8"
Island

Stepped Clg.

Her
WIC

His
WIC

bookshelves

P

Bath

CL

L

make-up

Foyer

CL

L

Master Bath

Whirlpool

Porch
20'-8" x 8'-0"

Bedroom 1
12'-8" x 11'-8"

CL

1ST FLOOR

From the fish-scale siding to the dormers, this delightful façade grabs your attention. The substantial great room features a coffered ceiling, built-ins and open access to the kitchen and dining rooms. The great room and study share a double-sided fireplace, and both rooms boast French-door access to the rear porch — as does the sizeable master suite. Calandre also features a luxurious master bath, bonus room and more.

3 Bedroom / **2** Bath

Living Area: **2,454** sq ft

Bonus Room: **256** sq ft

Width: **80'8"**

Depth: **66'0"**

Exterior Walls: **2x6**

Foundation: crawl space

Price Code: **C2**

REAR ELEVATION

AUBERRY | 7069

Auberry's gorgeous window dormer has been specifically placed to bring natural light into the welcoming foyer. Stepped and tray ceilings define this open, bright floor plan that features a private master suite with luxury bath; generous dining and great rooms with multiple sets of French doors to the back porch; kitchen with useful eating bar; and, above the garage, a bonus room offering many possible options.

3 Bedroom / **2** Bath

Living Area: **1,616** sq ft

Bonus Room: **362** sq ft

Width: **64'0"**

Depth: **55'0"**

Exterior Walls: **2x6**

Foundation: crawl space

Price Code: **C1**

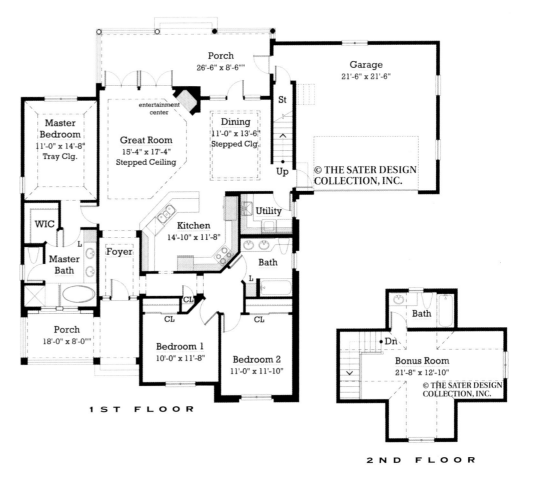

Porch
26'-6" x 8'-6"

Garage
21'-6" x 21'-6"

Master Bedroom
11'-0" x 14'-8"
Tray Clg.

entertainment center

Great Room
15'-4" x 17'-4"
Stepped Ceiling

Dining
11'-0" x 13'-6"
Stepped Clg.

St

Up

© THE SATER DESIGN COLLECTION, INC.

WIC

Master Bath

Foyer

Kitchen
14'-10" x 11'-8"

Utility

Bath

CL

CL

CL

Porch
18'-0" x 8'-0"

Bedroom 1
10'-0" x 11'-8"

Bedroom 2
11'-0" x 11'-10"

1ST FLOOR

Bath

Dn

Bonus Room
21'-8" x 12'-10"

© THE SATER DESIGN COLLECTION, INC.

2ND FLOOR

Product Gallery

Innovative solutions from Whirlpool Corporation

When it comes to appointing your Dan Sater signature home, you should not stop short of perfection. The cabinets, surfaces, appliances, and lighting you choose will contribute to the overall enjoyment of your home, its value now and in the future, and reflect your personal style. Attractively designed and featured to exceed your expectations, the portfolio of brands from Whirlpool Corporation offer a compelling solution for any lifestyle in the kitchen, outdoor space, laundry, and even the garage. For cooking, food preparation and clean-up performance that ranges from classic to contemporary, the portfolio of brands offers a multitude of options to suit your styling preferences and functional needs.

KitchenAid Home Appliances, with its Architect Series of appliances, allows you to truly tailor your kitchen to your specific lifestyle needs. From the undercounter wine cellar to single-drawer dishwashers, KitchenAid offers a suite of appliances that brilliantly perform the specialty tasks that you require.

Jenn-Air Home Appliances has been an industry leader in ventilation and cooking technologies for years. With appliance suites using innovative technology and finishes that entice your imagination, the Euro-Style Floating Glass, Stainless Steel and Oiled Bronze product lines offer an array of styles to match any décor. All of these choices from Jenn-Air mean you don't have to sacrifice performance for style.

Whirlpool Home Appliances, with the Whirlpool Gold Brand, brings increased efficiency and productivity to your traditional kitchen and laundry space. Innovative features like FastFill Technology, PowerScour™ cleaning, SpeedCook technology, and Direct Inject Wash Systems save you time and effort.

Maytag Home Appliances has stood long as a brand recognized for its strength and durability. High-end finishes and innovative offerings like the Ice_2O ice dispensing system and EPIC laundry pair distinguish this brand both in the marketplace and in your home, while its legacy of durability inspires confidence in performance.

Gladiator® GarageWorks rounds out the entire home offering by maximizing storage and workspace in the garage with style. By moving things up and off the floor, the Gladiator® GarageWorks system allows you to use that garage space to store cars again, or for any activity that is important to you.

KitchenAid Architect Series II

The Architect® Series II is an evolution of performance and intuitive design that will capture the attention of all your senses. We've combined the best of our original Architect® Series with a host of enhancements, offering an enticing suite of kitchen appliances inspired by, and created for, those who love to cook and entertain. The timeless appearance of the Architect® Series II comes in the form of robust contoured knobs, rounded corners, and seamless stainless-steel edges. Efficient performance is reflected in adjustable settings, intuitive displays and control graphics with complementary features designed to work together for a smooth cooking experience.

KitchenAid Home Appliances

Thoughtful innovations that are essential in the avid cook's kitchen

Outdoor Products

Throughout its long history, KitchenAid has remained true to its roots as the brand for those that love to cook. From chopping your fresh ingredients to rinsing the last of your stemware, every product and innovation that carries the KitchenAid name is designed with a single goal: to be an essential ingredient in every cook's kitchen.

Our full-line of countertop and major appliances includes outdoor appliances that extend our reputation for exceptional performance. Whether you're looking for a grill or an entire outdoor kitchen, we have mouth-watering solutions that will keep your guests coming back for more. Built-in or freestanding grills feature even cooking performance. Additions such as an outdoor refreshment center, refrigerator, and ice maker help you to keep your essential ingredients conveniently close, and add even more flexibility to your outdoor entertaining.

Built-In Outdoor Kitchen

Shown above is a built-in variant of the KitchenAid Outdoor Kitchen, a principal component of any outdoor entertaining space.

New Freestanding and Built-In Grilles

Shown below is an example of the new Commercial Series Grilles that will be available in 2007 from KitchenAid. A full-line of matching outdoor products is planned to replace the current product line-up.

KitchenAid ®

FOR THE WAY IT'S MADE.®

Jenn-Air Kitchen Suites

Traditional or avant-garde. Elegant or urban. Romantic or maverick. Whatever your style, there is no better place to express it than in your home...especially the kitchen. What more is style, after all, than a true expression of your individuality?

They say that beauty is in the details, and this is especially true of Jenn-Air® appliances. Details designed for both beauty and functionality. The curve of the handle on a wall oven, the placement of the vent on a downdraft cooktop, or the smooth glide of the freezer drawer on a French door refrigerator...all designed to work with you at the height of your creativity.

Choose to feature products individually or group them together for a complete ensemble. The possibilities are vast, and the results are inspiring. Express your own Jenn-Air® style.

Whirlpool® Home Appliances

For busy, active people who appreciate help in accomplishing their tasks and managing their homes, Whirlpool® and Whirlpool Gold® Brands are sure to fit your demanding lifestyle. Appliances that meet your everyday needs, are easy to use, reflect your individual tastes and help you to be incredibly productive. Whether it is part of a solution for the Kitchen or the Laundry Space; Whirlpool Brand products unite style and performance—offering innovative solutions that enable you for everyday chores, while saving time, managing space and achieving results with less effort.

Maytag Home Appliances

For generations, families have depended on Maytag® products in the laundry room. Today you can count on us for a full range of quality laundry and kitchen appliances with features designed to help you handle the demands of busy life. Maytag's commitment to innovation is unsurpassed with industry firsts such as: the Gemini® oven, the first double oven range; Ice$_2$O,™ the first ice-through-the-door French Door refrigerator; and the first full 3rd rack dishwasher. Feel confident in built-to-last appliances for your home without sacrificing premium performance by choosing Maytag.

Gladiator® GarageWorks

Gladiator® GarageWorks organization systems do more than lift items off the floor and hide the mess from your neighbors. Gladiator transforms your garage into a welcoming and usable room of your house—a place to work, entertain and show off to your friends and neighbors. Created by Whirlpool, the full line of Gladiator workbenches, storage solutions, appliances and accessories have all the details you expect from one of the most trusted names in your home—and a few features that might surprise you. Rugged, tread-plated steel construction. Heavy-duty casters. Maple tops. A refrigerator than keeps your beverages icy in summer, but not frozen in the winter.

Sleek. Rugged. Refined.

Country Estates Index

Blueprints

WHAT'S IN A SET?

Each set of plans is a collection of drawings that show how your house is to be built. The actual number of pages may vary, but most plan packages include the following:

A-1 COVER SHEET/INDEX & SITE PLAN

An Artist's Rendering of the exterior of the house shows you approximately how the house will look when built and landscaped. The Index is a list of the sheets included and page numbers for easy reference. The Site Plan is a scaled drawing of the house to help determine the placement of the home on a building site.

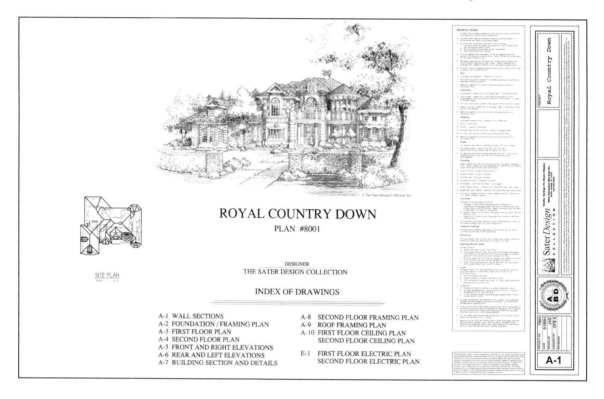

A-2 WALL SECTION / NOTES

This sheet shows details of the house from the roof to the foundation. This section specifies the home's construction, insulation, flooring and roofing details.

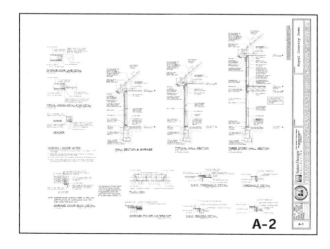

A-3 FOUNDATION PLAN

This sheet gives the foundation layout, including support walls, excavated and unexcavated areas, if any, and foundation notes. If the foundation is monolithic slab rather than basement, the plan shows footing and details.

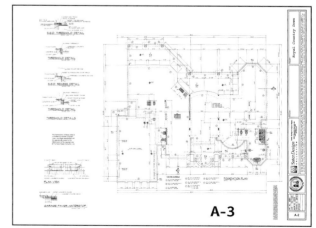

A-4 DETAILED FLOOR PLANS

These plans show the layout of each floor of the house. Rooms and interior spaces are carefully dimensioned and keys are given for cross-section details provided later in the plans, as well as window and door size callouts. These plans also show the location of kitchen appliances and bathroom fixtures, etc.

A-5 CEILING PLAN

Sater ceiling treatments are typically very detailed. This plan shows ceiling layout and extensive details.

A-6 ROOF PLAN

Overall layout and necessary details for roof construction are provided. If trusses are used, we suggest using a local truss manufacturer to design trusses to comply with your local codes and regulations.

A-7 EXTERIOR ELEVATIONS

Included are front, rear, left and right sides of the house. Exterior materials, details and measurements are also given.

A-8 CROSS SECTION & DETAILS

Important changes in floor, ceiling and roof heights or the relationship of one level to another are called out. Also shown, when applicable, are exterior details such as railing and banding.

A-9 INTERIOR ELEVATIONS

These plans show the specific details and design of cabinets, utility rooms, fireplaces, bookcases, built-in units and other special interior features, depending on the nature and complexity of the item.

A-10 SECOND FLOOR FRAMING

This sheet shows directional spacing for floor trusses, beam locations and load-bearing conditions, if any.

E-1 ELECTRICAL PLAN

This sheet shows wiring and the suggested locations for switches, fixtures and outlets.

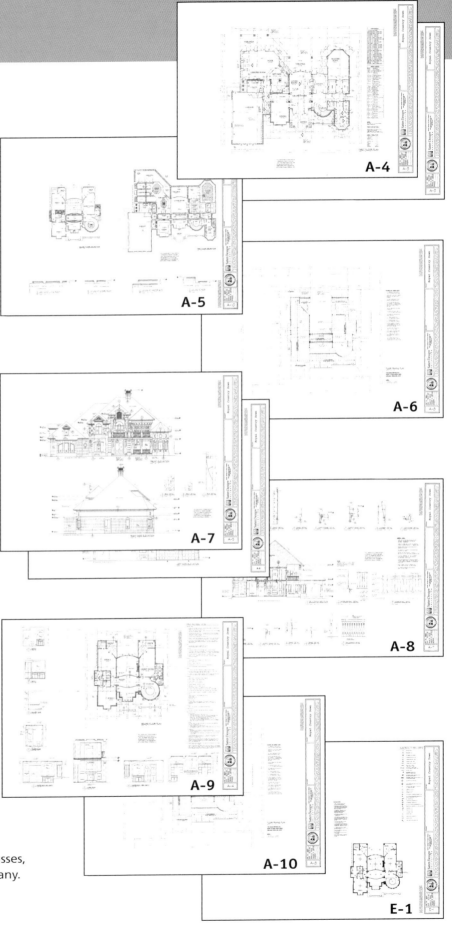

QUICK TURNAROUND

Because you are placing your order directly, we can ship plans to you quickly. If your order is placed before noon EST, we can usually have your plans to you the next business day. Some restrictions may apply. We cannot ship to a post office box; please provide a physical street address.

OUR EXCHANGE POLICY

Since our blueprints are printed especially for you at the time you place your order, we cannot accept any returns. If, for some reason, you find that the plan that you purchased does not meet your needs, then you may exchange that plan for another plan in our collection. We allow you sixty days from the time of purchase to make an exchange. At the time of the exchange, you will be charged a processing fee of 20% of the total amount of the original order, plus the difference in price between the plans (if applicable) and the cost to ship the new plans to you. Vellums cannot be exchanged. All sets must be approved and authorization given before the exchange can take place. Please call our customer service department if you have any questions.

LOCAL BUILDING CODES AND ZONING REQUIREMENTS

Our plans are designed to meet or exceed national building standards. Because of the great differences in geography and climate, each state, county and municipality has its own building codes and zoning requirements. Your plan may need to be modified to comply with local requirements regarding snow loads, energy codes, soil and seismic conditions and a wide range of other matters. Prior to using plans ordered from us, we strongly advise that you consult a local building official.

ARCHITECTURE AND ENGINEERING SEALS

Some cities and states are now requiring that a licensed architect or engineer review and approve any set of building documents prior to construction. This is due to concerns over energy costs, safety, structural integrity and other factors. Prior to applying for a building permit or the start of actual construction, we strongly advise that you consult your local building official who can tell you if such a review is required.

DISCLAIMER

We have put substantial care and effort into the creation of our blueprints. We authorize the use of our blueprints on the express condition that you strictly comply with all local building codes, zoning requirements and other applicable laws, regulations and ordinances. However, because we cannot provide on-site consultation, supervision or control over actual construction, and because of the great variance in local building requirements, building practices and soil, seismic, weather and other conditions, WE CANNOT MAKE ANY WARRANTY, EXPRESS OR IMPLIED, WITH RESPECT TO THE CONTENT OR USE OF OUR BLUEPRINTS OR VELLUMS, INCLUDING BUT NOT LIMITED TO ANY WARRANTY OF MERCHANTABILITY OR OF FITNESS FOR A PARTICULAR PURPOSE. Please Note: Floor plans in this book are not construction documents and are subject to change. Renderings are artist's concept only.

HOW MANY SETS OF PRINTS WILL YOU NEED?

If you are planning to obtain estimates from a contractor or subcontractor, or if you are planning to build immediately, you will need at least five sets. Because additional sets are less expensive, make sure you order enough to satisfy all your requirements. Sometimes changes are needed to a plan; in that case, we offer vellums that are reproducible and erasable so changes can be made directly to the plans. Vellums are the only set that can be reproduced; it is illegal to copy blueprints. The checklist below will help you determine how many sets are needed.

Plan Checklist

_____ **Owner** (one for notes, one for file)

_____ **Builder** (generally requires at least three sets; one as a legal document, one for inspections and at least one to give subcontractors)

_____ **Local Building Department** (often requires two sets)

_____ **Mortgage Lender** (usually one set for a conventional loan; three sets for FHA or VA loans)

_____ **Total Number of Sets**

IGNORING COPYRIGHT LAWS CAN BE A
$1,000,000 *mistake!*

Recent changes in the US copyright laws allow for statutory penalties of up to $150,000 per incident for copyright infringement involving any of the copyrighted plans found in this publication. The law can be confusing. So, for your own protection, take the time to understand what you cannot do when it comes to home plans.

WHAT YOU CANNOT DO!

YOU CANNOT DUPLICATE HOME PLANS
YOU CANNOT COPY ANY PART OF A HOME PLAN TO CREATE ANOTHER
YOU CANNOT BUILD A HOME WITHOUT BUYING A LICENSE

SATER DESIGN COLLECTION, INC.

25241 Elementary Way, Suite 201
Bonita Springs, FL 34135

1-800-718-7526

www.saterdesign.com

sales@saterdesign.com

ADDITIONAL ITEMS

15x22 Color Rendering Front Perspective* $195.00
(Suitable for framing)

Material List C1-L4 . . . .$150.00

Material List PSE5 . . . .$350.00

Additional Prints (per set) $65.00

Reverse Mirror-Image Prints $50.00

*Call for availability. Special orders may require additional fees.

POSTAGE AND HANDLING

Overnight $54.00

2nd Day $43.00

Ground $33.00

Saturday $74.00

For shipping international, please call for a quote.

Order Form

LICENSE PRICE SCHEDULE

	PRINT	CAD (Electronic)
C1	$.60 p.s.f.	$1.10 p.s.f.
C2	$.60 p.s.f.	$1.10 p.s.f.
C3	$.60 p.s.f.	$1.10 p.s.f.
C4	$.80 p.s.f.	$1.40 p.s.f.
L1	$.80 p.s.f.	$1.40 p.s.f.
L2	$1.00 p.s.f.	$1.70 p.s.f.
L3	$1.00 p.s.f.	$1.70 p.s.f.
L4	$1.25 p.s.f.	$2.00 p.s.f.
PSE5	Call for pricing	

* Prices subject to change without notice

p.s.f. = Price per square foot of total living area

Print License = Choice of six Print sets or one
reproducible Vellum

CAD (Electronic) License = One AUTOCAD™
compatible disk (if available)

PLAN NUMBER _____

☐ 5-set building package . . . . $_____

☐ 8-set building package . . . . $_____

☐ 1-set of reproducible vellums . . . . $_____

____ Additional Identical Prints @ $65 each $_____

____ Reverse Mirror-Image Prints @ $50 fee $_____

Sub-Total $_____

Shipping and Handling $_____

Sales Tax (FL Res.) 6% $_____

TOTAL $_____

Check one: ☐ Visa ☐ MasterCard

Credit Card Number _____

Expiration Date _____

Signature _____

Name _____

Company _____

Street _____

City _____ State_____ Zip_____

Daytime Telephone Number (_____)_____

Check one:

☐ Consumer ☐ Builder ☐ Developer

MEDITERRANEAN
LUXURY HOME PLAN BOOK

DAN SATER'S MEDITERRANEAN HOME PLANS

65 Mediterranean-style floor plans

In this unmatched portfolio of more than 65 unique home plans you will experience Mediterranean design in a new realm — one that delights, challenges and encourages the imagination. Superb architectural detail infuse sun-baked courtyards and loggias, while open floor plans stretch the boundaries of traditional Mediterranean style.

2,700 to over 8,000 sq ft

$14.95   *192 full-color pages*

COTTAGES & VILLAS
COASTAL HOME PLAN BOOK

DAN SATER'S COTTAGES & VILLAS

80 elegant cottage and waterfront home plans

A photo tour of 8 stunning coastal homes previews a portfolio of eighty beautifully rendered and charming clapboard cottages and grand Mediterranean villas. These highly versatile designs are big on open porches and courtyards, while balancing function with style, and bring to mind a relaxed attitude that can only come with view-oriented living.

1,200 to over 4,300 sq ft

$14.95   *224 full-color pages*

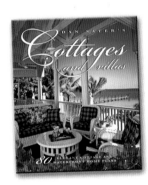

DAN SATER'S LUXURY
HOME PLAN BOOK

DAN SATER'S LUXURY HOME PLANS

Over 100 view-oriented estate homes

A colorful and richly textured collection of more than 100 exquisite floor plans. This stunning display of unique Sater homes features more than 220 pages of exciting interior and exterior photography, with unique design ideas for the most gracious living. Whether you're seeking plans for a 6,000-square-foot estate or a 3,000-square-foot villa, you can find them in this truly inspirational portfolio of Dan's best luxury home plans.

2,700 to over 8,000 sq ft

$16.95   *256 full-color pages*